MW00772720

ETERNITY IN THE
MIDST OF TIME

WILFRID STINISSEN, O.C.D.

Eternity in the
Midst of Time

~

Translated by
Sister Clare Marie, O.C.D.

IGNATIUS PRESS   SAN FRANCISCO

Original Swedish edition:
Evigheten mitt i tiden
© 1992 Libris, Örebro

Unless otherwise indicated, Scripture quotations are from Revised Standard Version of the Bible—Second Catholic Edition (Ignatius Edition) copyright © 2006 National Council of the Churches of Christ in the United States of America. All rights reserved worldwide.

Cover art:
Cupola of Genesis (composite photograph)
View of the dome with the Creation
Photo credit: Cameraphoto Arte, Venice/Art Resource
and
Close up of the center
Photo credit: Alfredo Dagli Orti/Art Resource, New York
Mosaic of the narthex,
Venetian Masters, ca. 1230
San Marco, Venice, Italy

Cover design by Enrique J. Aguilar

© 2018 by Ignatius Press, San Francisco
All rights reserved
ISBN 978-1-62164-280-0
Library of Congress Control Number 2018961114
Printed in the United States of America ∞

Contents

Preface

We think we know what time is. For as long as we have existed we have lived in it. We are familiar with time. Time is our home. We cannot imagine how it would feel to find ourselves outside of it.

But as soon as we begin to think about time, it becomes difficult. Perhaps no one has formulated it as clearly and strongly as Saint Augustine (354–430): "What then is time? If no one asks me, I know; if I want to explain it to someone who does ask me, I do not know."[1] Is it not strange that something as ordinary as time is so mysterious? As soon as we begin to go deeper into the essence of time, we find ourselves face to face with a mystery.

For many, it is surely rather annoying not to be able to understand something as simple as time. For myself, I prefer to rejoice in the fact that everything around us is so great and mysterious that we can live in eternal wonder and always philosophize more. We are like children in a land of fairy tales where everything is exciting and exploration never ends.

The intention of this book is not to explain what time is and thus take away its mystery. Instead, I would

[1] *The Confessions of Saint Augustine*, trans. John K. Ryan, bk. 11, chap. 14, no. 17 (Garden City, N.Y.: Image Books; Doubleday, 1960), 253.

like to begin with admitting that the simple reality of time surpasses my ability to understand it. My aim is to focus on time, to see it from different perspectives, to discover how rich and many faceted it is. Rather than take away its mystery, which would be arrogance, I would like to show that time is even more mysterious than we had imagined. Above all, I would like to examine how we should *live in time* and how we can make use of the tremendous possibilities that time offers to us.

I

The Riddle of Time

There can be a tendency to imagine time as something absolute, that there is a time that is valid for the entire universe. We associate it with the image of a ticking clock, of running water, or of sand; this time is the same for everyone; it lives its own life; it continues inexorably and independently of what we desire or do. We cannot prevent time from passing. It pays no heed to us.

Objective and Subjective Time

In reality, there is no absolute time. Time always has to do with something else: an event, a state of being, an action, a meeting. Aristotle's (384–322 B.C.) ingenious definition of time as "a measure of movement" joins the concepts of time and movement. Without movement, there is no time.

But time does not measure movement as a measuring stick measures a piece of cloth. The measuring stick remains always the same. But it is not so with time. Movement influences time, not only subjective time, but even so-called objective time, that is, clock time.

According to Einstein (1879–1955), we know that the speed of time varies, depending on how man moves in the universe. Time on earth goes more quickly than time in space. Scientists claim that if we could build a spacecraft with a speed that came close to the speed of light and that had no need of refueling, the first five years in the space craft would be comparable to almost seventy-five years on earth. When the astronauts came home after their long journey, they would be considerably younger than their children. If one wishes to lengthen his life, it would be wise to make a long and fast journey through space![1]

If we remain on earth, there is a time that we can call *objective* time. That is the quantitative time that we read on our clocks and to which we must adapt if we want to live in harmony with one another. This time, which is dependent on the turning and rotation of the earth, may not be underestimated. How could we have encounters with each other if there were not a universally valid time?

Still, it is not the quantitative time that is the most interesting, nor is that the time we will primarily be considering here. What interests us is subjective, psychological, experienced time.

The expression "subjective" time can perhaps awaken unpleasant feelings. Shall we really focus on analyzing subjective impressions and experiences? Would it not be better to keep to objective reality? Surely it would,

[1] Cf. Peter Nilson, *Tiden och universum i Människan och Tiden* (Västergötlands Turistråd: Skövde, 1989), 12.

but we must not confuse "objective" with "objectivistic". Philosophers have often had the tendency to think objectivistically; that reality is just what it is, *independent of man*. The ideal for the philosopher is to be an observer, to remain neutral, without interfering in reality's way of being. This leads, consequently, to a mechanical philosophy, to a reality that is like a machine. Let us see what this machine produces.

This kind of philosophy is uninteresting. Philosophy is only exciting when it helps us to *live*. It is always life that is primary and most important. All that does not contribute to our living a richer, more genuine life is worthless.

Reality Exists Thanks to Man

What does reality mean *for me?* Do *I* have a place in reality, and if so where? What is *my* purpose in reality? It is questions like these that philosophers worth their name ought to answer. The philosopher is not separated from the reality he is studying. He is a part of it; he influences it, enriches it, and gives it a new meaning.

While in the past, positive science was seen as the ideal for objectivity, the new physics shows that such an objectivity does not exist, that it is even, in principle, impossible. In quantum physics there is no sharp distinction between the one who observes and what is observed. The electron is either a wave or a particle, depending on how one places his instruments.

When I look up the definition of the word "mountain" in my dictionary, I find: "a natural elevation of the earth's surface". That is a typically objectivistic way of seeing it. In reality, a mountain is much more than a natural elevation of the earth's surface. A mountain is something you can climb, a place where you breathe cleaner air, where you feel a little closer to heaven, where you can pray better . . .

A stream is more than "a flow of water in a channel or bed". We get our drinking water from a stream. You can swim and bathe in a stream; you can lie on its shore and sunbathe; you can sit and meditate on the shortness of life. Thanks to the human person, this stream has a meaning that it could not have had before the arrival of man. It is these meanings that make the stream important for us, and, more than that, they allow the stream to "exist" and form its essence. Without man, the stream is only matter—one is tempted to say "dead matter", but we can hardly say this now in the era of new physics, since the border between life and non-life is more and more blurred—but when a person comes in contact with the stream, it becomes filled with meaning, sense, and spirit. It is precisely this meaning, this spirit that is the "substance" of a thing. "It is the Spirit that gives life, the flesh is of no avail" (Jn 6:63).

I do not think it is too presumptuous to quote these words here. Jesus said them just when he had openly spoken about the Eucharist. The disciples were astonished and did not understand how the bread that he would give them could be his Flesh. Nor has the Reformation been able to understand how the Catholic Church can speak of transubstantiation. How can one claim that the Eucharistic bread has been transformed into the Body of Christ when any scientist can prove that the bread has the same chemical makeup after the Consecration as it had before? Nothing has changed chemically. How then can the bread's substance have become the substance of Christ's Body? But the substance of things is not their chemical makeup. Rather, it is now the true Bread, the living Bread, the Body of Christ, that nourishes the divine life within us.

The "Talents" of Time

The purpose of this long digression was to show that "subjective", experienced time is not a less important time. It is rather the "objective", neutral time that is less important. Apart from the human person, reality is an incomplete symphony.

When God created the earth; he gave it to man so that he would "till it and keep it" (Gen 2:15). God presents all living beings to Adam "to see what he would call them; and whatever the man called every living creature, that was its name. The man gave names to all cattle, and to the birds of the air, and to every beast of the field" (Gen 2:19). To give a name is not only to demonstrate what the object consists of, as when a doctor diagnoses an illness and gives a name to it. Name-giving in the Bible is a creative process.

When God asks man to give a name to reality, he invites him to participate in his work of creation, to be his co-creator.

In the biblical perspective, the earth is created for man. The whole creation process tends toward the human person. When God placed the crown on his work and created man, he gave him charge of ruling over the whole earth (Gen 1:26). By his way of cultivating and making use of the earth, man gives it its purpose and completes the work of creation.

Naturally, man may not make use of the earth however he pleases. He may not "give a name" to things in a whimsical fashion. He must take into consideration the latent possibilities of things. Just as man has been given "talents" (Mt 25:14–30), so everything created has received its talents, and it is man's responsibility to bring forth these talents in the proper way.

Time also has its "talents".

What I wish to do here is examine how we can make these talents bear fruit, how we can make the neutral "clock time" become good time.

Cyclical and Linear Time

In ancient cultures, we find primarily a cyclical understanding of time. Time is an eternal cycle. The seasons of the year succeed each other, always in the same order. The sun goes up, and then it goes down; the new moon comes and then the full moon; day follows night, and night follows day. Time leads nowhere; there is no development, no goal, no end.

Ecclesiastes has adopted this eternal repetition. It is difficult to find a better description of the cyclical concept of time than this: "What has been is what will be, and what has been done is what will be done; and there is nothing new under the sun. Is there a thing of which it is said, 'See, this is new'? It has been already, in the ages before us" (Eccles 1:9–10).

Ecclesiastes is not representative of the biblical concept of time, however. In contrast to its contemporary culture, what is characteristic of the Bible is that it considers time as a frame for a historical, linear occurrence. There is a sacred history that has its origin in God's plan and is dependent on it. History has a beginning and an end. God wills something for his people. Something new is happening. "A new heart I will give you, and a new spirit I will put within you" (Ezek 36:26).

The prophets try to vaccinate their countrymen against their neighbors' culture of the cyclical concept of time by repeating that the passage of time has a mysterious goal, that they are moving toward something great: "For behold, I create new heavens and a new earth; . . . be glad and rejoice for ever in that which I create" (Is 65:17–18).

When God finally enters into history himself in Jesus, it is the great "good news". He comes to accelerate history's speed and make everything new (Rev 21:5).

The fact that the Bible prioritizes the linear concept of time does not mean that the cyclical concept is totally rejected. On the contrary, it is taken up and integrated into the linear concept. The cyclical element has an important place in the Church's liturgy: feasts recur, the psalms of the Liturgy of the Hours are divided up according to a timetable that is constantly repeated . . . One might even see the entire history of salvation as one great "cycle", where in the end God becomes as real for man as he was when he walked with him in the garden in the cool of the evening (Gen 3:8). Between paradise and heaven, the circle is closed.

Instead of speaking of linear time, we should perhaps speak of spiral time. The spiral is a synthesis of the cyclical and the linear. Everything returns, and yet everything is new, since it happens on a higher level. The key to a true life is precisely in beginning again with a whole new and fresh openness and, at the same time, with a foundation and starting point from previous experiences. The monotonous daily schedule of the contemplative, monastic life is a typical example of this "spiral life": the same thing is repeated again and again, but it leads always to new depths.

Man begins again and again, and every new beginning can be a new attempt, a new movement upward.

As We Are, So Time Is

These words of Saint Augustine are well known: "Bad times, hard times, this is what people keep saying. . . .

We are the times. Such as we are, such are the times."

There are as many experiences of time as there are people. And with every person the experience of time constantly changes. The experience of time is a kind of barometer by which we can read how man relates to reality. When we think that reality is boring, time goes slowly. The minutes creep forward, and time is then experienced, not as a gift, but as a curse.

We actually feel better "when we do not concentrate" on time. It fulfills its role best when it can stand in the background. As soon as we focus on it, it risks becoming our enemy. If we wish to experience time in all its length, without stepping over one second, then time becomes unbearable.

In his book *The Plague*, Albert Camus gives, with ingenious irony, a good recipe for not wasting one's time.

> *Query*: How contrive not to waste one's time? *Answer*: By being fully aware of it all the while. *Ways in which this can be done*: By spending one's days on an uneasy chair in a dentist's waiting-room; by remaining on one's balcony all of a Sunday afternoon; by listening to lectures in a language one doesn't know; by traveling by the longest and least-convenient train routes, and of course standing all the way; by lining up at the box office of theaters and then not buying a seat; and so forth.[2]

---

[2] Albert Camus, *The Plague*, trans. Stuart Gilbert (New York: Vintage Books, 1991), 26.

Time is not made to be experienced directly. Its function is to accompany us discreetly, without drawing attention to itself.

One could describe different types of people from the experiences of time that characterize them. Each one has his own personal way of living in time. One person is calm and seems to have an ocean of time; another is always nervous and stressed; there is never enough time. One experiences time as varied; everything is moving and constantly changing; another has an experience of unity and stability in the midst of change.

These different ways of experiencing time are one of the reasons it is so difficult for us to live together. For some people, things do not go quickly enough; time is insufficient. "For heaven's sake, get moving", they sigh. Others, on the contrary, think there is no reason to hurry; they always have an endless amount of time. The collision between these opposite ways of living in time is an inexhaustible source of conflict.

Some experience time as negative, as a waste. Ecclesiastes is one of them. He certainly does not have a positive view of time.

> The sun rises and the sun goes down,
>   and hastens to the place where it rises.
> The wind blows to the south,
>   and goes round to the north;
> round and round goes the wind,
>   and on its circuits the wind returns.

All streams run to the sea,
  but the sea is not full;
to the place where the streams flow,
  there they flow again. . . .
The eye is not satisfied with seeing,
  nor the ear filled with hearing. . . .

I have seen everything that is done under the sun; and behold, all is vanity and a striving after wind. (Eccles 1:5–8, 14)

Some, on the other hand, see time above all as an opportunity, a possibility, a challenge. Time gives us an occasion to do something, to develop. In contrast to Ecclesiastes' pessimistic view, the prophets are more optimistic. They point to a bright future: something is going to happen, let us look forward to this, let us prepare ourselves!

A typical example of someone with the optimistic view of time was Pope John XXIII (1881–1963). On one occasion, at the solemn commencement of the Second Vatican Council, he said in a memorable speech: "We feel bound to disagree with these prophets of doom who are forever forecasting calamity—as though the world's end were imminent. Today, rather, Providence is guiding us toward a new order of human relationships, which, thanks to human effort and yet far surpassing human hopes, will bring us to the realization of still higher and undreamed of expectations."[3]

---

[3] October 11, 1962, in Thomas Cahill, *Pope John XXIII* (New York: Penguin Books, 2008), xi.

There are people who prefer to live in the past—the elderly, as we know, have a tendency to live in their old memories—others live primarily in the future, and a small number of people live in the present moment. We all relate to the three dimensions of time in our own typical way.

The experience of time also has to do with culture. Different cultures mean different time. In the industrialized world, time goes more quickly than for people who live closer to nature. Europe and the United States have a different time from that of India. For us, time represents work and, therefore, money. To lose time is to lose money, and money stands for a standard of living, well-being, happiness.

We are children of our time, whether we like it or not. The environment and the culture in which we live influence us. It is important to be conscious of our point of departure, so that we understand to what degree our experience of time is conditioned by our milieu. Only when we have a clear view of our starting point can we make an assessment of it. We can consciously consent to the time our culture tries to impose on us, or we can reject it.

We can choose the time we wish to have. Or rather, we can choose the time that God wants to give us. We can only live in harmony with him and with ourselves when we wholeheartedly consent to the time God has decided for us. And without harmony in ourselves, we have no possibility of living in harmony with others.

The Meaning of Time

Why did God create time? Why must we live in this strange life with its many difficulties and sufferings, with its sins and mistakes, before eternity's door opens for us? If God is love, if he is so generous, why does he not give us everything at once? Why must it take such a long time before we reach our goal?

God himself lives outside of time, in an eternal now, in a beatitude where nothing is lacking to him. If it is his will—as Christianity claims—that we participate in his life, why does he not allow us to enter immediately into his bliss? Why must we take such an endless number of small, faltering steps, where we often risk making wrong ones?

Time to Grow

Many philosophers have marveled over this strange situation in which man has been placed. Man longs for the absolute, for wholeness, and, in practice, he attains only small fragments. Everything in his life must happen gradually.

He cannot even completely be himself. One can say of God that he is himself, that he is totally contained within himself. But man must leave himself in order to find himself. He does not recognize himself completely in what he is right now. Instead of being complete in himself, he is fragmented: he is pulled simultaneously toward the past and the future. He lives as though he were scattered abroad, as in a diaspora. One could even say he *is* a diaspora.

It is his task to transform this multiplicity into a structured unity.

But why does God give man such an "impossible" task? Why does he not create him complete from the beginning? In my small book *Into Your Hands, Father*, I have tried to explain why God did not create man perfect.[1]

It is not because he wanted to make life difficult for him but, rather, because he, in his love, wants to give him the possibility of participating in his own Trinitarian life. The life of the three Divine Persons consists of an eternal giving to and receiving from each other. If man had been created perfect from the beginning, he would certainly have taken part in the three Persons' receiving of each other, but not in their giving. He would have received everything from God, but he would not have been able to "give" him anything. In this way, he would have lost out on an essential aspect of love. For love always means giving and receiving.

---

[1] Wilfrid Stinissen, *Into Your Hands, Father*, trans. Sister Clare Marie, O.C.D. (San Francisco: Ignatius Press, 2011), 72–75.

In reality, man is *not ready* when he comes forth from the hands of God. He endows him with capacities that he must realize himself. He gives him a free will so that he can freely choose or reject him. That is the meaning of the forbidden tree in the creation narrative: God places the first human couple before a definitive choice. If they choose God, they have *done* something for him, *given* him something. Then God is happy and thankful. He does not wish to have a monopoly on generosity or to force man into a one-sided gratitude. He wills for man to be generous, also, and he himself wants to be grateful.

But to choose God in order to realize one's potential, to develop and mature and thus *become* complete, requires time. The purpose of time is precisely so that we can develop and grow.

Compared to eternity, time can seem inferior, degenerate. But this is an abstract speculation. If we look at man's purpose and destiny, which is to be introduced into the life of the Trinity, then it is clear that time is a gift. Time gives us a chance to grow. Thanks to time, what God has placed within us can germinate and become a tree. Because of time, we have the possibility of participating in God's creation ourselves.

There is a grain of truth in the claim of Jean-Paul Sartre (1905–1980) that man is a creature that chooses himself. He is, of course, chosen by God, but God also gives him a chance to make choices himself. What he is when he dies is different from what he was when he was born, and what he has become is partly the fruit of his own effort, his own "merit". We are perhaps allergic to that word in a predominantly Protestant culture, but maybe it is time to rediscover its rich meaning.

God Reveals Himself in Time

We can conclude that time is something good from the fact that God has revealed himself in time. Time is spoken of both in the beginning and at the end of the Bible. The Bible begins with: "In the *beginning* God created the heavens and the earth" (Gen 1:1) and ends with: "Surely I am coming soon" (Rev 22:20). The entirety of revelation is placed within time.

That God creates *in the beginning,* means that there is no time before creation. God exists outside of time. Time *begins* when God creates. The Bible immediately establishes that God is transcendent, that we cannot contain him in categories of time and space. There is no time before creation in which God would have lived and developed. Time always has to do with creation. If God had never created, there would never have been time.

The seven days show that creation is a process. God creates it one day after the other. It takes time, and it is good that it takes time to complete creation. In the Bible, time is not an illusion from which man must free himself, as Gnosticism and certain oriental religions claim. It is God himself who lays the foundation and establishes time by not creating everything at once, but in stages. Time is holy, time has a religious significance, because it has its origin in God's work of creation.

It is enough to read the creation account to understand that there cannot be a radical disharmony between time and eternity. Since God who is eternal and transcendent creates time himself, it must have something of eternity in it.

It is true that this eternal dimension of time has been partially lost through the Fall. It becomes the mission of Jesus and each one of us to "redeem" time (Eph 5:16; Col 4:5).

Not only creation, but the whole of revelation takes place in time. The Old Testament is the long story of God's slow revelation. When he wishes to reveal himself, he does not come with a treatise where everything is there from the beginning. We do not receive a synthesis, where all that he wishes to communicate about himself and us is systematically explained. No, he reveals himself through events. Noah is saved from the Flood; Abraham is called to leave his country; Moses is saved from death as a newborn; Israel is led out of Egypt; God takes care of his people in the desert, and he leads them into the Promised Land. It is by doing something for and with his people that God shows who he *is*.

The great temptation for Israel is not being able to wait until God reveals who he is but, instead, making idols for themselves and consequently deciding for themselves who God is. The one who makes an idol can decide for himself how it will look and what characteristics he will ascribe to it. But God wills that we respect time. After all, how could he reveal himself totally at once; "truly, you are a God who hide yourself" (Is 45:15), a God whose "greatness is unsearchable" (Ps 145:3). The little human being needs to receive revelation in small doses. To *see* God would result in death (Ex 33:20).

The purpose of the Old Testament is, among other things, to show that God has gone the long way when he wished to reveal himself to man. Time in the New Testament, on the other hand, is extremely concentrated. "I am the truth", Jesus says of himself (see Jn 14:6). He contains all truth in heaven and on earth. "He who has seen me has seen the Father" (Jn 14:9).

Just as the disciples are blinded on the Mount of the Transfiguration, we are also blinded by the light that radiates out from him. But just on Mount Tabor, where Jesus shows himself in glory, Moses and Elijah are also present. The entire Old Testament is present. The complete revelation does not fall suddenly and unexpectedly from heaven. It has a long history. And all of this history is there when Jesus finally crowns his work. "Do not think", he says, "that I have come to abolish the law and the prophets; I have come not to abolish them but to fulfil them" (Mt 5:17). Despite the fact that eternity enters into time in and with him, he does not deny time. He does not reject anything of what God has already said about himself from the very beginning of creation. It is just the opposite; he lets everything have its proper place. The time of the Old

Covenant is taken up into the fullness of time that is indicated by the New Covenant.

From the beginning, the Church has done as Jesus did. Though she knows that the New Testament really is a "new" covenant, she has continued to read the Old Testament readings in her liturgy. She has realized that these scriptures retain their value and are important for us in understanding something of God's pedagogy: how he patiently instructs his people.

In some way, even we, however much we live in the fullness of revelation, must go the whole way. The Old Testament is still relevant for us. The narrative of the exodus from Egypt is a permanent exhortation: we must also leave the slavery of Egypt and go out of ourselves to be led into the desert where God will educate and rear us. A preparation time is necessary in order to understand the good news and enter into it.

For all who long for the absolute and who in their eagerness have a tendency to want to leap over all the intermediate stages, it is healthy to read the Old Testament and learn the ways in which God reveals himself there.

Time Is God's Waiting for Us

The Romanian Orthodox theologian Dumitru Stăniloae explains how we can get insight into the deepest meaning of time only when we discover how it has its roots in God's own Trinitarian life.[2] Since man is

---

[2] *Dieu est amour* (Geneva: Labor et fides, 1980), 50–53.

created in the image of God, we can understand him only when we see him as a reflection of God's Triune being.

The Trinity is a dialogue of love between the Father and the Son. The Father gives all of his love, that is, himself, to the Son and waits for the Son to consent to this fundamental pattern that makes up the essence of love: I give myself and wait for you to receive me, and in the receiving you give yourself in return. In the Holy Trinity, there is an absolute immediacy: the Father's offer and the Son's response coincide perfectly. Their love is perfect. That is why there cannot be any doubt or delay between the question and the answer. Love's immediacy is God's eternity.

When God offers his love to us, it is different. He did not create us so that we would necessarily and automatically say Yes. What would a love of that kind be worth? He wants us to decide an answer willingly. He *waits* for our Yes. Time is just this length and breadth of waiting. "Do you want this?" God asks, and then he gives us "time" to mature toward a Yes.

Time is a sign of God's patience. One could say it *is* his patience, incarnate. "Behold, I stand at the door and knock" (Rev 3:20). The fact that he stands at the door and remains there is precisely what time consists of. Most people do not answer immediately when they hear God knocking. But God does not give up. He waits, and, by giving us time, he shows what a great price he puts on our answer.

For us to grow and mature means to make the time between God's knocking and our answering ever shorter. God invites us to come gradually closer to his own immediacy and so grow into his eternity.

A person who is totally deaf to God's communication, who is not at all interested in what he has to offer, deprives time of its meaning and makes it into absurd time. But he does not completely succeed, because God cannot help but continue to hope and wait endlessly.

Everything Has Its Time

It is truly not a curse that we must live in time. Many believe that time and eternity stand in direct opposition to each other. But this is not so. It is just by wholeheartedly entering into time, taking it seriously, and discovering its original meaning that we find eternity within it. Eternity is the innermost marrow of time. If time is used in the right way, it bears fruit, "and . . . your fruit should abide" (Jn 15:16).

Perhaps this is the most mysterious and fascinating aspect of time: we cannot imagine anything more fragile and fleeting than time, and yet it is completely filled with something that "abides". And it is just the one who totally accepts the fleetingness of time, who does not in the least way try to cling to anything but lets everything have "its" time, who is also the one whose fruit most "abides".

Do you feel how something of eternity's peace and stability come over you when you hear Ecclesiastes speak of the fleetingness of time?

> For everything there is a season, and a time for every
>   matter under heaven:
> a time to be born, and a time to die;
> a time to plant, and a time to pluck up what is planted;
> a time to kill, and a time to heal;
> a time to break down, and a time to build up;
> a time to weep, and a time to laugh;
> a time to mourn, and a time to dance;
> a time to cast away stones, and a time to gather stones
>   together;
> a time to embrace, and a time to refrain from
>   embracing;
> a time to seek, and a time to lose;
> a time to keep, and a time to cast away;
> a time to tear, and a time to sew;
> a time to keep silence, and a time to speak;
> a time to love, and a time to hate;
> a time for war, and time for peace. (Eccles 3:1–8)

In the growing process that is our life, there are many stages to reach, many steps to take, and fortunately everything has its time. Time is an asset. It gives us the possibility to develop without having to step over important phases in the process. For every step there is a season. And the reverse is also true: every moment of time that we receive is given to us so that we might grow a little more. Time is the possibility for growth.

Perverted Time

The modern man hardly needs to be reminded that time is an asset. That time is money is known by all. The question is if this calculated, quantitative perspective of time is not in direct opposition to what the purpose of time really is. There is surely nothing wrong with seeing that time *also* has a capacity for production. But if it is emphasized so much that in the end it defines the entire value of time, something is wrong.

If the employee is constantly pressured to increase the tempo of his work, if everything goes toward producing as much as possible in the shortest amount of time, then time becomes an evil force. Instead of giving the worker an opportunity to grow and become more alive, time is manipulated in such a way that it destroys all life. To force a person to work beyond his capacity without taking into consideration his individuality and personal rhythm is to block every possibility of development.

Jesus teaches us how we should work: "Let your light so shine before men" (Mt 5:16). As natural as it is for light to shine, it ought to be equally natural for us, as the light of the world, (Mt 5:14) to spread light through our work. It presupposes that this work comes from within, that there is a contact between our work and the center of our being, that work is allowed to take the time that it takes.

When I say that time is an asset, I mean something more than "time is money." To identify time with "dishonest mammon" is to pervert it. Jesus says that in eternity mammon will desert us (Lk 16:9). If time is used to gather mammon, it is deprived of its eternal dimension. By definition, mammon is something that passes away. " 'Fool! This night your soul is required of you; and the things you have prepared, whose will they be?' So is he who lays up treasure for himself, and is not rich toward God" (Lk 12:20–21).

In the final analysis, everything depends on how we understand the development of man. Is man only on a journey toward death (Martin Heidegger, 1889–1976), or is he on a journey toward life? To invest time in money, to make use of it to amass possessions, makes life a journey toward death. For when the hour has come, not only is everything taken away from us, but the collection of material possessions bears within itself the mask of death.

To seek the meaning of life in something that lies outside of us, something that, in addition, is extremely fragile, only increases our feeling of alienation and rootlessness. Inner growth is exchanged for a horde of material things. What a terrible waste of time!

"Instead, seek his kingdom, and these things shall be yours as well", says Jesus (Lk 12:31). Everything material is there for the taking, precisely as much as we need. When we direct our energies toward inner growth, that which is a surplus becomes a nuisance.

And inner growth is to seek "his kingdom", that is, God's love.

God wants to give us his love, and he created time so that we would little by little open ourselves to it.

And Yet All at Once

Again we can ask the question: Why does God not give *all* of his love at once; why must it take such a long "time"?

In reality, God *does* give all at once. There is no hesitation on his part, no delay. He cannot wait. At baptism he gives us his Holy Spirit, and in and with him, he gives us everything at once.

But *we* need time in order to open ourselves up to this gift and, through our own little contribution in cooperation with God, to build up the mutual relationship of love between him and us for which we were created.

Saint John of the Cross (1542–1591) has a striking text about this dissimilarity in time (*temps*) with God and man. "The espousal made on the cross is not the one we now speak of. For that espousal is accomplished immediately when God gives the first grace that is bestowed on each one at baptism. The espousal of which we speak bears reference to perfection and is not achieved save gradually and by stages. For though it is all one espousal, there is a difference in that one is attained at the soul's pace, and thus little by little, and the other at God's pace, and thus immediately."[3]

Imagine if we could learn something about the discipline of time that we find in the "children of this world"! Every second is given to us in order to grow into the love we have already received. Time is the environment, the divine environment that is appropriate for all who have not yet *reached* perfection but are in the process of *becoming perfect*.

Not to *become* is to be unfair to time, to deprive it of its meaning.

But for the one who knows that it is a question of *becoming* what he *is*, time is filled with eternity.

3

Jesus' Time

A real theology of time naturally flows from Jesus' own life.

If God has become man in Jesus, it is to show how one lives a human life while being God and how we can live a divine life while being human.

Even if Jesus' situation is unique, since he unites two natures in *one* person and can say of himself: "Before Abraham was, I am" (Jn 8:58), there is still an analogy between his attitude and ours. We are "partakers of the divine nature" (2 Pet 1:4); we are grafted onto him as branches on a vine (Jn 15:5).

In *The Spiritual Canticle*, Saint John of the Cross explains how the soul in the state of union is able to "thoroughly understand the profound and eternal mysteries of [the] Incarnation, which is by no means the lesser part of beatitude".[1] One of these mysteries is "union with this divine wisdom, Who is the Son of God [as well as] the sublime mysteries of God and human

[1] Saint John of the Cross, *Spiritual Canticle* 37, 1, in *The Collected Works of Saint John of the Cross*, trans. Kieran Kavanaugh, O.C.D., and Otilio Rodriguez, O.C.D. (Washington, D.C.: ICS Publications, 1991), 614.

beings".[2] There was a greater unity between Jesus and us than we imagined. This unity wants to express itself in our concrete way of living.

Pure Openness to the Father

According to Hans Urs von Balthasar (1905–1988), Jesus' time is that "very constitution of his being, by which it is perpetually open to receive his mission from the Father".[3] Jesus' time is determined and defined by the fundamental words he speaks about himself and that one could write as a motto for his life: "For I have come down from heaven, not to do my own will, but the will of him who sent me" (Jn 6:38). It is repeated as a refrain in the Gospel of John that the Son receives everything from the Father. "Truly, truly, I say to you, the Son can do nothing of his own accord, but only what he sees the Father doing; for whatever he does, that the Son does likewise. For the Father loves the Son, and shows him all that he himself is doing" (Jn 5:19–20; cf. 5:30; 12:9–50).

Jesus does not speak in his own name; he does not attribute anything to himself. "The words that I say to you I do not speak on my own authority; but the Father who dwells in me does his works" (Jn 14:10).

But the Father is not in him as though he were in an empty house. Despite the fact that Jesus does

[2] Ibid., 37, 2, p. 615.

[3] Hans Urs von Balthasar, *A Theology of History*, 2nd ed. (San Francisco: Ignatius Press / Communio Books, 1994), 33–34.

not do what he himself wills, he does have his own will: "Father, I *desire* that they also, whom you have given me, may be with me where I am" (Jn 17:24; emphasis added). Jesus is not the Father's loudspeaker. He himself is involved and engaged to the highest degree. He has his own personality, his own "I". He can even say: "I am" and thereby claim to share God's name. But he is what he is by receiving it from the Father.

He receives everything in such a way that it becomes his own, to which he can freely have recourse. "No one takes [my life] from me, but I lay it down of my own accord. I have power to lay it down, and I have power to take it again" (Jn 10:18). But then he continues, "this charge I have received from my Father" (ibid.). Even this, to distribute freely what he has received, is a gift from the Father. He has received his entire being from the Father, and it is this that makes up his identity. If he should forget for one instant that all he is and has comes from the Father, he would not be the Son. And then he would not be credible (Jn 10:37).

We know that everything Jesus says and does as man on earth reveals what he is within the Holy Trinity. His existence on the earth is a translation in human terms of what he is as the Father's Son in eternity. He is the one who receives himself from the Father in eternity. His existence is an existence of receiving. He is "born of the Father before time began". His life on earth expresses that and makes it visible.

Those who see him live and act and who truly *want* to see and hear understand that he receives both his being and acting from the Father.

Jesus is not a human being who is already programmed in advance and then *later*, in another instance, opens himself to the Father and receives his mission from him. No, he *is* openness, receiving, obedience. That is his essence. There is nothing in his being, either in his thinking or acting, that falls outside of this turning toward the Father.

"His being as self", writes Hans Urs von Balthasar, "never becomes a theme (and thus inevitably a problem) but only passes, down to its very roots, into prayer."[4] This prayer is "Abba! Father!"

Jesus does not wish to have exclusive rights to this "turning toward the Father". "And because you are sons, God has sent the Spirit of his Son into our hearts, crying, 'Abba! Father!' " (Gal 4:6). He wills that, by grace, we should be what he is by nature: a prayer. Even here his words apply: "I have given you an example, that you also should do as I have done to you" (Jn 13:15).

By instituting the Eucharist, he shows that it is deadly serious for him. Here one is as far removed from self-centeredness as one can be. To make oneself food and drink, to let oneself be eaten and drunk, is the complete opposite of what we in our time so readily call "self-realization". Does our self-realization not

[4] Ibid., 32.

seem a bit ridiculous when we are confronted with the Eucharist?

Jesus Has Time

Time is also received by Jesus from the Father. He knows that time is part of the life of man. Man has received the mission to be fruitful and multiply, to fill up the earth and master it (Gen 1:28). It does not happen at once; it takes time. When Luke writes that "Jesus increased in wisdom and in stature" (2:52), he is saying by this that Jesus respected time. He was not in a hurry. He could wait until the "time" was right. This is also abundantly clear from his unusually long, hidden life in Nazareth.

We, on the other hand, are, in practice, inclined to deny time. We try to step over time, make decisions that we are not ready to make, and carry out tasks that have not been given to us.

Was this not the very sin in paradise, that man could not wait until the fruit was given to him? We read that the one who is victorious shall eat from the tree of life (Rev 2:7). But man cannot wait that long. He greedily seizes the fruit and eats both of the wrong tree and at the wrong time.

Every sin is fundamentally a rejection of time. Everything good comes from God, but he does not give everything at once. Sin is to want to have something that God does not yet wish to give, to seize immediately what he wishes to bestow only gradually.

"When you eat of it [the forbidden tree]", says the
serpent to the woman, "your eyes will be opened, and
you will be like God, knowing good and evil" (Gen
3:5). It was, in fact, a part of God's plan that man
should become like him. But the time was not yet
right. He wanted man to prepare himself for this gift,
to develop and grow into this. But man did not have
the time.

Not to have time, that began already in paradise!
Man boldly assumes the right to be like God. He does
not want to hear about any postponement or delay.
He rejects the long maturation process that belongs to
time.

So we understand why the New Testament speaks
so insistently about patience. It is a question of waiting, of staying awake, of being prepared (Mt 25:1–
13). We cannot go into the wedding feast whenever
we wish, but only when the bridegroom comes (Mt
25:1–13). "Behold, I am coming like a thief!" says
Jesus, "Blessed is he who is awake, keeping his gar-
ments that he may not go naked and be seen exposed!"
(Rev 16:15).

Jesus is aware of the fact that there is an "hour" that
he may not bring about in advance. "O woman, what
have you to do with me? My hour has not yet come"
(Jn 2:4). This hour of his is also his Father's hour. It is
this hour when he will be victorious and glorified by
his suffering and his death. He does not want to have
any power over this hour or even to know when it will

come: "But of that day or that hour no one knows, not even the angels in heaven, nor the Son, but only the Father" (Mk 13:32).

It is by this voluntary unknowing that he remains open to and dependent on the Father. The hour comes when the Father allows it to come. It is enough that the Father knows. There is in him no curious searching into the future. The future will come when it comes. And when the hour finally comes, it is completely new and fresh. It is not broken into pieces by preconceived ideas, musings, or expectations.

Not to take something in advance is characteristic of Jesus' way of living in time. He receives what is given by the Father. And the Father gives him what he needs to know and do in order to carry out his mission.

In the past, it was thought that Jesus had a detailed knowledge of all that he had to do and of all that could happen during his life. Not to have this knowledge would, of course, mean that he was not God. When the opposite claim is made today, namely, that Jesus was unaware of much of what was to happen, it is often because of a lack of faith in God.

Jesus *is* God, but an *incarnate* God. He takes seriously that he has become man, and he wants to be like us "in all things but sin".[5] He freely relinquishes his divine knowledge and lays it in the safekeeping of the Father. In this way, he does not become less but

[5] The Fourth Eucharistic Prayer in the liturgy of the Catholic Mass, cf. Heb 4:15.

shows even more that he is God: he reveals even more clearly who God is. God is love, who gives of himself totally for the sake of the beloved.

Precisely because of the fact that Jesus, of his own free will, does not know everything that will happen to him, he can be our model of faith, "the pioneer and perfecter of our faith" (Heb 12:2), and also tell his parables about staying awake and waiting in uncertainty. He does it himself!

Real and Unreal Time

For Jesus, time is not an empty vessel that he can fill with something he chooses for himself. His time is always filled. It coincides with the mission he has received from his Father. For him to have time means to have time for God. His time is the Father's time. This time does not stand in opposition to eternity. On the contrary, it is filled with eternity: the action of the Father becomes present in time. This time is grace. This time is always the right time, salvation's time (2 Cor 6:2).

Alongside the real time, there is also an unreal time, a time that misses the goal, a time that is "lost". This time is sin's or the sinner's time, a time when one, like Jonah, flees from God and his mission. This time is not filled with eternity, since God refuses to enter into it. In this time, nothing happens. Or we could say, it is filled with hopelessness and meaninglessness. "Remember", writes Saint Paul, "that you were at that time separated from Christ . . . and strangers to the covenants of promise, having no hope and without God in the world" (Eph 2:12).

But nothing is definitively lost, since Jesus integrates even unreal time, distorted time, into his own time. He himself goes through meaninglessness on the Cross, not because he turns away from his Father and says No to his mission, but just because he has received as his mission to live through the meaninglessness of unreal time and, in that way, give a meaning to meaninglessness itself.

The time that was "lost", when all is said and done, does not need to be lost. Just as Jesus takes the lost lamb on his shoulder, he also takes the lost time onto himself and makes it the Father's time. "Where sin increased, grace abounded all the more" (Rom 5:20).

All time is encompassed in Jesus' time. God gathers everything together in him (Eph 1:10).

"I Am the Alpha and the Omega" (Rev 1:8)

Jesus' time does not only have a height and a depth through which he, in a vertical relationship to the Father, at every moment lets himself be sent by him. His time also has a length and a width. It extends out from the present moment to the right and to the left. He does not only stand in the midst of time, but he is master over time from beginning to end.

Everything that came before Jesus pointed to him. By constantly doing and saying what the Father shows him, he fulfills all the promises and prophecies. The entire Old Covenant, all that was foretold, finds its fulfillment in him.

Jesus knows the Law and the Prophets. He knows that they speak of him (Jn 5:39). When he reads the text from Isaiah in the synagogue in Nazareth: "The Spirit of the Lord is upon me, because he has anointed me to preach good news to the poor", he adds without the slightest doubt: "Today this Scripture has been fulfilled in your hearing" (Lk 4:18, 21). He explains for the disciples on the way to Emmaus: "beginning with Moses and all the prophets, . . . in all the Scriptures the things concerning himself" (Lk 24:27).

The Old Testament texts do not belong only to the past. They mark out the way that Jesus must go. How often do we read: "For the Scriptures had to be fulfilled. . . . This happened so that the Scriptures would be fulfilled"? Jesus must become "like a lamb that is led to the slaughter, and like a sheep that before its shearers is silent" (Is 53:7). And by the fact that Jesus lets himself be crucified without any resistance, he becomes that lamb and "fulfills" the prophecy.

It seems as if Jesus is not free to do what he wills. He may not deviate from what is written. "Do you think that I cannot appeal to my Father, and he will at once send me more than twelve legions of angels? But how then should the Scriptures be fulfilled, that it must be so?" (Mt 26:53–54).

In reality, Jesus' freedom is not limited by these prophecies. The truth is not that he must give his life for the people because it is written, but it is written because the Father wills that he should give his life and because Jesus consents to the Father's will.

It is Jesus who is the norm. That he fulfills the Law and the Prophets does not mean that he is dependent on them; it means that the Law and the Prophets are dependent on him. He stands sovereignly within time and reigns over the past. It is his life that forms and characterizes the Law and the Prophets.

Just as he rules over the past, he also rules over the future. He is "the fullness of time". When he says: "It is finished" (Jn 19:30), in a certain sense, time reaches its climax. That for which time had been created, to give man the opportunity to mature and reach his final destiny, had already found its perfection in Jesus.

What we call the future will not add anything radical to what Jesus has done. The role of the future is only that we shall "believe in" what has once been done. In the same way, the sacrifice of the Mass is not anything "new", either, but is rather an actualization of what Jesus has done "once for all" (Heb 9:12).

In all its brevity—thirty years—Jesus' time sums up and encompasses all of man's time. Everything that comes before and after him is included in his time. By summing up all time in himself, he can redeem time from its slavery to corruption (Rom 8:21) and fill it with eternity.

4

Christian Time

There is a specific Christian time. Christians live differently in time from the way non-Christians do. The transition to Christianity always entails a transition to a new time.

This new time is so different that it is really a question of a break with the past. Saint Paul speaks of a "before" and a "now": "Formerly, when you did not know God, you were in bondage to beings that by nature are no gods; but now that you have come to know God, or rather to be known by God, how can you turn back again to the weak and beggarly elemental spirits, whose slaves you want to be once more? You observe days, and months, and seasons, and years!" (Gal 4:8–10). Saint Paul is addressing those who trusted in the ancient astrology that distinguished between favorable and unfavorable times. For a Christian, however, time is always favorable.

But the fact that Christian time is new does not mean the old, natural time is set aside. The old is taken up into the new and undergoes a transfiguration, just as the Old Testament is transformed by the New, or as the bread in the Eucharist is transformed into "the true Bread", the Body of Christ.

The Specific Feature of Christian Time

What distinguishes Christian time from all other time is that it is completely characterized by Jesus' time. In Christian time, Jesus' time continues. It is not as though the time of a Christian is completely identical to Jesus' time. There is something in his time that is unique and characteristic of him. But it is nevertheless Jesus' time that gives the Christian's time its physiognomy. If we wish to know how we as Christians should relate to time, we can turn to Jesus and see how he lived in time.

1. Just as time was *a gift from the Father* for Jesus, who gave him the possibility of carrying out his mission, it is the same for us. The Father creates time and gives it to us. Therefore, time is good. We ought to be thankful for all the time we receive. A Christian knows that he does not control time, that he cannot take it or seize it. A Christian who is twenty years old does not take it for granted that he has fifty years left. Every moment is a *gift*.

The time that God gives always involves a mission. The time we are given is not an empty jar that we are free to fill or not. There is no empty time in the Bible. The word "time" always has a complement that implies the reason why time is given: a time to eat, a time to work, a time to sow, or a time to harvest [see Eccles 3]. There is never any time to waste. The fact that God gives us time means: you have something to do. And above all: you have something to become.

We will not be unemployed in heaven. The great occupation in heaven will be to worship God and sing "Holy, holy, holy" (Rev 4:8). But there are occupations that can only be carried out here on earth by people who live "in time". God needs hands and feet, eyes and ears, mouths and tongues, in order that the good news shall be proclaimed and transformed into reality. If certain people are not prepared to let themselves be used, God is in some sense powerless.

2. What most characterizes Christian time, however, is the total *transformation* time has undergone through the Incarnation. Before the Incarnation, time was only time, a time without wholeness, divided up into past time, present time, and future time. After the Incarnation, time is mixed in a mysterious way with eternity. God has entered history, the eternal has been transplanted into what is perishable.[1] And therefore also the reverse: time has entered into eternity; history now touches God's own life. This mysterious mixture of time and eternity does not end when Jesus dies on the Cross. It continues in his disciples, who live from his life. For all of us, it is a question of being eternal beings while being bound by time; that we live both *in* time and stand *above* time.

---

[1] Nikolai Berdyaev (1874–1948), *The Meaning of History*, trans. George Reavey (1936; New York: Routledge, 2006), 68.

The fragmentation of time in the past and the future, where the "future is the murderer of every past instant",[2] disappears when one goes in search of one's roots. Time is no longer only something that races past, something limited and that soon comes to an end. Time is filled with eternity.

A Christian is actually never "in search of the time that has passed". There is no time that has merely "passed". The eternity that has entered into time gives it a unity that keeps it from passing away. For a Christian, the past is not only what is no longer real, and the future is not only that which is not yet real. The past and the future are concentrated in the present moment.

The radical dualism between time and eternity, where eternity stands for what is stable, lasting, and total, and time stands for what is unstable, passing, and partial, is conquered in Christian time. Eternity places its stamp on time.

Let us look closer at this.

The Presence of the Past as Grace

The past exists in the present moment, not as a destructive power, but as a source of praise and thanksgiving. The past is often experienced as the time of irrevocable and irreparable mistakes. The decisions of the past have limited and perhaps destroyed my possibilities. My now is marked in an awful way by what was in the past. It feels as though I no longer have any

[2] Ibid., 70.

freedom, since everything I do must follow the path that my past has marked out. My past has an alienating power: I cannot be myself since I live under the tyranny of my past.

This is not so for a Christian. All the negative in my past is forgiven, and, in the forgiveness, the minus has been transformed into a plus. Now I can give thanks for my mistakes and sins. In and through them, God's mercy becomes living for me. And the consequences of my sins, which continue to influence and guide my life externally, are transformed into God's grace-filled will; a will that I need not seek with difficulty but that is given to me.

It is no longer meaningful to try to sort out what happened in the past and distinguish between positive and negative. Everything becomes positive, everything becomes grace when one goes through one's life and sees it with Christian eyes; everything is illuminated and transfigured, and only "God's mercy" remains: or in man's heart and mouth the words: "praise the LORD! . . . for he is good" (Ps 106:1).

When Saint Teresa of Avila (1515–1582), in a letter to Canon Don Pedro de Castro y Nero, tells about her autobiography, where she describes in detail her sins and lack of faith, she says that she has given the book the title *De las Misericordias de Dios* (Of the mercies of God).[3]

---

[3] Saint Teresa of Avila, *The Collected Letters of Saint Teresa of Avila*, November 19, 1581, vol. 2 (Washington, D.C.: ICS Publications, 2007), 480.

Saint Thérèse of Lisieux (1873–1897) does the same. When she begins her *Story of a Soul* she writes: "I'm going to be doing only one thing: I shall begin to sing what I must sing eternally: '*The Mercies of the Lord*'."[4] In another context, I have pointed out that in this text Saint Thérèse gives proof of a healthy memory, that rather than looking at her own sins and weaknesses, she remembers *God's* work.[5] One could also speak of a *Christian* memory. A Christian, by definition, lives more in Christ than in himself. When he remembers his past, he does not remember primarily what he himself has done. He remembers "the mercy of the Lord".

It makes no difference if one has a long or a short past. Since the time of a Christian is permeated by eternity, one can learn as much in a few years as during a long life. Saint Thérèse laughs at the very common habit of judging experience by one's age:

> For a very long time, I have known that this way of measuring experience according to years is practiced among human beings. For instance, the holy King David has sung to the Lord: "*I am YOUNG and despised.*" And in the same Psalm 118, he does not hesitate to add: "*I have had understanding above old men, because I have sought your will . . .*" [v. 100]. You did not hesitate, dear Mother, to tell me one day that God

[4] Saint Thérèse of Lisieux, *Story of a Soul: The Autobiography of Saint Thérèse of Lisieux*, trans. John Clarke, O.C.D., 3rd ed. (Washington, D.C.: ICS Publications, 1996), 13.

[5] Wilfrid Stinissen, *Into Your Hands, Father*, trans. Sister Clare Marie, O.C.D. (San Francisco: Ignatius Press, 2011), 44.

was enlightening my soul and that He was giving me even the experience of *years*.[6]

She says to her Sister Marie du Sacré-Coeur a few months before her death that she is a baby who has deep thoughts, "un bébé qui est un viellard" (a baby who is elderly).[7]

The Presence of the Future in the Now

When we look toward the future, we see that it is also concentrated in the present moment. The future is not something unknown, frightening, threatening, or terrible that can strike me at any moment. No. "I know whom I have believed" (2 Tim 1:12). I know that he has laid his hand on me and that nothing can separate me from the love of Christ (Rom 8:35). Nothing evil can happen to me because that which God has begun will also be brought to perfection. He is faithful. He is my rock.

For the unevangelized person, the future is something toward which he is moving. Man goes in the direction of his future. He wants to conquer and seize it, "manufacture and form it". It is a question of thinking of one's future and concentrating his energies on it. His whole life is spent securing and guaranteeing his future.

---

[6] Saint Thérèse of Lisieux, *Story of a Soul*, 209–10.

[7] Saint Thérèse of Lisieux, *Derniers entretiens* (Paris and Bruges: Desclée de Brouwer, Éditions du Cerf, 1971), 443.

A Christian, on the other hand, does not move toward the future, but the future comes to him. It is not
man who comes close to God's kingdom, but God's
kingdom that comes close to man (Mk 1:15). And in
the prayer of the Our Father we do not say: "we come
to your kingdom", but "your kingdom come" [*adve-
niat regnum tuum*].

Theologians distinguish between *futurum* and *adventus*. *Futurum* is the future of the secularized man, the
future that is in large part the fruit of our own labor.
Adventus, on the other hand, is the time of the Christian, the future that is coming. *Adventus* is the future
that we do not need to create but that is given to us
from above. We cannot elbow our way into the future, into God's kingdom, but God's kingdom is like
the holy city Jerusalem that is "coming down out of
heaven from God" (Rev 21:10).

We do not need to run toward the future. The future comes to us itself. Not a threatening future, but a
glorious, blissful one, because our future is God. This
revolutionizes both our concept of time and our whole
way of living.

In a paradoxical way, the future does not exist completely in the future but is rather, in a certain way,
contained in the present moment. Christian hope is a
divine blend of "already" and "not yet".[8] The essential has already happened. We are pardoned. We are
already children of God.

---

[8] Vatican Council II, Dogmatic Constitution on the Church
Lumen Gentium (November 21, 1964), no. 48.

God has already "raised us up with him [Christ]" (Eph 2:6). We already live in the end times (1 Jn 2:18). The eschatological time is in progress *now*. We pray that God's kingdom will come, but at the same time we know that it already has. God's kingdom is in our midst and within us (Lk 17:21).

The present moment is therefore not a fleeting point between the past and the future, a moment that continually slips away and that we can never grasp. The present moment is charged with both the past and the future. The present is a concentration of all of time's dimensions. The two seemingly unreal and elusive dimensions of time (the past and the future) are completely and fully real in the present. *Our now is the incarnation of God's eternal, timeless now.* The present is God's "today", as the Letter to the Hebrews says (3:7—4:11).

Time for a Christian does not mean fragmentation but, instead, wholeness, fullness. When we live as Christians in the present moment, we receive everything at once, "*as it was in the* beginning, is now and ever shall be".

The Trinitarian Quality of Time

From all of this we can conclude that time bears a completely Trinitarian stamp. Just as there are three Persons in God, so time is made up of three dimensions.

The *past* relates to the *Father*. He is the origin, the beginning. You are created by him, born of him, sent by him. In him you have your roots.

We find the *future* in the *Son*. He is one with his mission. He *is* the Word. He is in the process of gathering all that was dispersed (Jn 11:52) in order to place it under his feet (1 Cor 15:27), to build up the kingdom of the Father. What he has done "once and for all", he is in the process of revealing in its perfection. He will return to judge the living and the dead. He is our ideal, our future.

Just as the *Spirit* unites the Father and the Son and is the bond of love between them, the *present* also unites the past and the future. The Spirit is your rule at every moment, just as he once was for Jesus. He inspires you and makes the Father's mission concrete, moment by moment. He adjusts himself flexibly to your *present* situation.

And as theologians speak about the *circumincessio* of the three Divine Persons, that they go in and out of each other, so there is also a *circumincessio* when it is a question of the three dimensions of time. The past, the present, and the future live in and penetrate each other. All is in all.

5

Prayer—To Stand
before the Eternal One

There is a royal road for the one who wishes to discover eternity in time: namely, prayer.

In prayer we turn ourselves directly toward God, and we know that the past and the future converge in him in an eternal now. To open oneself to God is to open oneself to eternity.

But do we really open ourselves to God when we pray? There is a way of praying where we do not really leave our prison, when we only ask God to make our prison a little more comfortable. As long as prayer is limited to praying for money, success, or a larger apartment, there is no chance we will enter into eternity.

Jesus does indeed teach us to pray for our daily bread. But before we reach this part of the Our Father, we have already hallowed his name and prayed for his kingdom to come and that his will may be done. Jesus himself gives the petition for daily bread a subordinate place. If we pray that prayer, it is not because we are distressed that there may not be enough bread but, rather, because we wish to remind ourselves that we are dependent on our Father in heaven for everything.

To make progress in prayer means that we pray for the most essential things. "Therefore do not be anxious, saying, 'What shall we eat?' or 'What shall we drink?' or 'What shall we wear?' For the Gentiles seek all these things; and your heavenly Father knows that you need them all" (Mt 6:31–32).

A Single Pray-er: The Spirit

When Jesus tells the parable of the man who asks his friend to lend him three loaves of bread in the middle of the night and points out that perseverance is rewarded, he adds unexpectedly: "If you then, who are evil, know how to give good gifts to your children, how much more will the heavenly Father give the Holy Spirit to those who ask him!" (Lk 11:13). He implies discreetly that what the Father wants to give us most of all is the Holy Spirit.

The only need we have is the need for the Holy Spirit. If we have him, prayer becomes incredibly simple. We no longer need to worry about what we shall pray about. We do not even know what is good for us. "We do not know how to pray as we ought, but the Spirit himself intercedes for us with sighs too deep for words. And he who searches the hearts of men knows what is the mind of the Spirit, because the Spirit intercedes for the saints according to the will of God" (Rom 8:26–27).

Our need for the Spirit *has* been fulfilled. "God's love has been poured into our hearts through the Holy

Spirit who has been given to us" (Rom 5:5). When we pray with the Church: "Come, Holy Spirit", it is not in the sense that the Spirit has been far away until now and shall finally come, but that he who has been given to us at baptism will fill our consciousness more and more. We wish to become conscious of his presence; we wish to understand how rich we are.

Prayer for the coming of the Holy Spirit can look like a demanding prayer, but it is fundamentally a prayer of thanksgiving. We learn to acknowledge the gift we have received. In this "acknowledgment", all questions of what we shall pray to God for are answered. The kingdom of God has come by the fact that the Holy Spirit has been given to us. And the Spirit is in himself the eternal one, the never-ending stream of love who is the *origin*, *end*, and *meaning* of our life in this existence limited by time.

In the deepest sense, there is only one pray-er: the Spirit. When we persevere in praying for him to come, he increasingly takes over the prayer within us. Prayer that had previously been a burden—because there was so much to pray for—becomes rest. We listen to him and assent to his prayer. We unite ourselves with his whispering: "Abba! Father!" (Gal 4:6).

The Spirit was present at the creation of the world: he hovered over the waters (Gen 1:2). He will also be there at the end of time: "The Spirit and the Bride say, 'Come'" (Rev 22:17). He "has filled the world" and "holds all thing together" (Wis 1:7). For him, history is not a chaotic event, and time is not a disintegrating force. Everything that is and that happens is one in him who leads history toward its goal.

To listen to him and rest in him is to find eternity in time. "He [God] has put eternity into man's mind", says Ecclesiastes (3:11). These words take on a whole new meaning when we know of the "living flame of love" that burns in the depths of our soul.

In this prayer, there is nothing to request, nothing to ask, and nothing to complain about. There is nothing more "to do" than "simply be", "to be—eternally in God".

Contemplative Prayer

What we experience of reality before we pray is above all its limitations. We experience how everything is passing and slipping away. But after prayer, we see how everything has an unlimited capacity to mediate God's glory. We ourselves are filled with eternity, and we discover eternity's dimension in everything.

"Well and good if all things change, Lord God, provided we are rooted in You", writes Saint John of the Cross.[1]

By making our dwelling place in God through prayer, we no longer live in what is changing. Things continue to come and go on the periphery, but we are no longer

[1] Saint John of the Cross, *Sayings of Light and Love*, no. 34, in *The Collected Works of Saint John of the Cross*, trans. Kieran Kavanaugh, O.C.D., and Otilio Rodriguez, O.C.D. (Washington, D.C.: ICS Publications, 1991), 88.

involved. We find ourselves on a deeper level, in God who is stability itself. There is hardly a quality in God that the Bible emphasizes more than his stability. In eternity, he remains unshakably the same.

The prayer of which I am speaking here is *contemplative* prayer. It is the prayer in which one does not wish to *have* or *receive* anything from God, but where one rests in him. It is the prayer Saint John of the Cross wishes to teach his readers. He considers it his foremost duty to lead people along the contemplative way.

> God gives many souls the talent and grace for advancing, and should they desire to make the effort they would arrive at this high state. And so it is sad to see them continue in their lowly method of communion with God because they do not want or know how to advance. . . . Some souls, instead of abandoning themselves to God and cooperating with Him, hamper Him by their indiscreet activity or their resistance. They resemble children who kick and cry and struggle to walk by themselves when their mothers want to carry them.[2]

Even in the beginning of *The Ascent of Mount Carmel*, Saint John shows how the ascent will happen. In order to be led all the way to the top of the mountain, I must surrender myself like a little child and rest in the arms that carry me.

To some extent, all prayer is directed toward contemplation, since the ultimate goal of all our striving

[2] Saint John of the Cross, *The Ascent of Mount Carmel*, prologue, no. 3, in *Collected Works of Saint John of the Cross*, 115.

and longing is to behold and worship God. But this must not be understood as though pure contemplative prayer is the only right way to pray. The prayer that corresponds to our needs and capacities right now is the right prayer for us. "Pray as you can, and do not try to pray as you can't", writes Abbot John Chapman (1865–1933) to a correspondent. Each one has the right to be completely himself before God, and anything else is actually a waste of time, since God sees us as we are anyway.

We pray out of our personal capacities. If we are sick, it is normal that our first thought is to pray for health. The Gospel shows us that God takes this prayer seriously. He really listens. But if this prayer is not answered as we had hoped, we begin to realize that health is not something absolutely necessary.

There are many things we think we need in order to be happy or in order to work for God's kingdom. By not always satisfying our desires, God leads our thoughts in new directions. He lets us see what is essential and frees us from a lot of dead weight. Eventually, he lets us see our real needs, our need for him. And if we faithfully follow his lead, we begin to realize that this basic need has been satisfied for a long time. God has given us himself. In the Eucharist, his total self-giving is an actual, visible, tangible, and edible reality.

Our prayer then receives a greater calmness and unity. It is no longer guided by the changes of time but, instead, has its roots in eternity, in the Eternal

One. Earlier we prayed for things. Now we say with the Psalmist: "One thing have I asked of the LORD, that will I seek after; that I may dwell in the house of the LORD all the days of my life, to behold the beauty of the LORD, and to inquire in his temple" (Ps 27:4). Earlier we prayed with anxiety, sometimes with anguish. We were not sure about God, not completely convinced that he would give us what we need. Now we know that he both can and will give us the very best and that, in reality, we have already received it. There is nothing to pray for since everything has already been given. We have abandoned all the partial goals and rest now in the goal that has already been reached.

This prayer is worship, thanksgiving, and praise. *Worship*, because we allow God to be God: he may decide; he may do exactly as he wills. *Thanksgiving*, because we like and accept beforehand what God does and is, and we receive him in complete openness. And *praise,* because we cannot give God greater homage than to trust him without reservation. It has become a prayer that is similar to what our unceasing occupation will be when this time on earth has passed.

Have You Come Farther Than You Think?

But once again: No one needs to pray in this contemplative way before he is ready for it. The question is only if you might belong to a higher level than you think. You may have more in you than you know. The Spirit prays in the deepest part of your being, even if you do not think you have come that far yourself. Do you dare to listen to his wordless sighs?

Certainly, not all are called to the same degree of contemplative prayer. Some are by nature more active and extroverted and are not capable of being still and quiet for long periods of time. But for many, it would be enough to have a little guidance and a bit of courage to discover a simpler prayer that would give them a deeper satisfaction and bring them nearer to God than their old way of praying could do. We are like fledglings that begin to fly, and when they have once taken flight, they feel they are in their element. We feel that this is what we were created for.

Is there anyone who does not wish, at least now and then, to withdraw for a moment from the activities and the clamoring din of time in order to rest in something eternal, unchanging, and firm? Something that gives coherence to all his occupations?

In this simple, contemplative prayer, we take the prayer of the Holy Spirit seriously. We know that since the moment we were baptized into the Trinitarian life, a Trinitarian prayer has been taking place in the center of our soul. This prayer is immeasurably deeper, "more serious", than the one we ourselves can "produce". Now, it is a question no longer of carrying out the prayer, but rather of *allowing* it to take place. "The Spirit helps us in our weakness" (Rom 8:26). Why should we reject that help? The only thing we should do is seek silence, exteriorly and interiorly, in order to perceive the Spirit's "voice without words". One is not able to hear his sighs if one is making a lot of noise himself. "Be still, and know that I am God" (Ps 46:10).

A Prayer for Our Time

A typical characteristic of this simple prayer is that one does not become tired of it. It is tiring to live in multiplicity. To live in unity is rest. The one who begins such a prayer enters into God's rest. That is why this prayer is a blessing for the weary people of our time. After a day's work, most people are too tired to practice meditation. But one is never too tired to rest! The only mishap that could befall us is that we would fall asleep. But is it not better to fall asleep in God's arms than to continue to hurry? This prayer is particularly a gift for those who devote themselves to intellectual work: it is good to be free from thinking and let one's tired head rest in God. All the scattered thoughts and feelings can disappear, while I, who am infinitely more than my thoughts and feelings—only rest, stretched out on the firm and eternal rock who is my Creator and God.

Perhaps someone will object that life in our day is too stressful, that we are bombarded with far too many impressions to be able to reach the inner stillness that is required for this contemplative prayer. This objection contains a dangerous trap. One blames the external situation to avoid taking oneself in hand. It becomes a comfortable excuse to avoid taking responsibility for one's own life. Can we not turn it upside down and claim that this noisy and stressful life that more than ever characterizes society today is precisely what impels us to seek a healthy compensation? Contemplative prayer can be a counterweight to the centrifugal forces of our time. With it, we can sow the "seeds" of eternity in our own hearts and the hearts of others.

To avoid all misunderstanding, I wish to underline that we are speaking here about prayer and not a sinking into ourselves. Prayer is a search for God, a search that is completely marked by love. And love always consists of both words and silence. That silence to which we give ourselves when we begin this still, simple prayer presupposes that we speak with God outside of prayer, listen to his word, and meditate on his love. Only then can silence in prayer be warm, rich, and genuine. Loving words are needed. But if they are not interrupted by or end in silence, something essential is missing. In the loving dialogue between two lovers, it is this silence that constitutes the high point of love.

What is to be done concretely? How can we get the thought engines to stand still? How can we calm the chaotic confusion that usually fills our poor heads? What do we do in order to come in contact with God's will and, thus, discover eternity in time?

I will describe some simple exercises. The disadvantage with them is that they are so simple that one has difficulty taking them seriously. We do not believe we can have any results with such simple means. We are familiar with the thought that results depend on the intensity of our effort. It is not so in this case. It is by the very simplest means that we reach our goal. It is not so unusual, since this is a question of reaching God, and no one is simpler than he is. We also know that as soon as we try to live according to the Gospel, which is God's message, life immediately becomes simpler.

The Prayer of Relaxation

The majority of us are stressed and tense. Perhaps we are not aware of our tensions. We can also draw a parallel with having a sense of sin. Many Christians have not the faintest idea of their egoism, but as soon as they begin to seek God seriously, their egoism also becomes manifest. It is greater than they thought and can even seem insurmountable. It is the same with our tensions. Only when we work with them do we begin to see how deeply rooted and stubborn they are.

Why is it so important to do something about our tensions? Because tension is essentially an existential lack of openness. "Be opened", Jesus says (Mk 7:34). Just as blood flows through our veins freely and easily and as air fills our lungs and supplies the whole body with oxygen, in the same way, God, who lives in the center of our soul, wishes to fill our whole being and activate our powers with his life. If we are tense, it hinders not only our blood circulation and breathing, but it also makes it more difficult to receive God's love.

Man is a whole. His physical form expresses who he is. Tension, as a rule, points to some deficiency in our surrender. Old and painful experiences are perhaps not completely accepted but repressed. We have still not said a wholehearted Yes to reality, to life, to God. Or else in our self-willfulness we wish to carry out our plans without taking into consideration time and our own strengths and weaknesses.

Through surrender, we open what was closed. We say Yes instead of No. What psychologists call "acceptance", we Christians call "surrender". We not only accept reality, we surrender it to someone else: to God and his love.

There is a surrender prayer that engages our entire being. It becomes extremely concrete by the fact that it allows the body to participate in the prayer. The body is allowed to pray in its own way in that it systematically relinquishes its tensions and in this way says its own Yes to God.

While you now and then repeat: "I surrender to you, Father", you go through the body, from the bottom upward or from the top downward, and let go, let go. You let the eyes say "Yes, Father", and the cheeks, the mouth, the throat, and the shoulders . . . You open yourself more and more to God's peace, which now flows not only into the soul but also into the body.

After a while, you feel perhaps that you have attained peace, that now you only wish to rest in God. And you do that. But then you become distracted again, and then it can be wise to open yourself to God again via the body.

This prayer has the advantage of making you less sub-

ject to distractions, the great pitfall in all contemplative prayer. Contemplation can easily degenerate into
drowsiness. Here you have a concrete task: to travel
through the body and surrender to God in every part
of your body.

Many tensions are so deeply rooted that they are not
released immediately. It does not matter. You say Yes
to this also. You surrender as much as you can. Not
more and not less.

Breathing Prayer

In the creation narrative, we read that the Lord God
breathed the breath of life into man's nostrils and that
man thus became a living being (Gen 2:7). Breathing is
placed on a footing with life. The Person of the Trinity whom we call the "Life-Giver" is called the "Holy
Spirit". When Jesus wishes to impart the Holy Spirit,
he breathes on his disciples (Jn 20:22). Breathing, life,
and the Holy Spirit point to each other.

As a rule, breathing is unconscious. But it can become conscious. And it can become prayer. Feel how
you breathe. Feel how the air comes into the nostrils
and through the windpipe into the lungs. Feel how the
warm air goes out the same way again, to leave room
for the somewhat colder air that now comes in. Follow this continuously out and in. You know that every
breath means life, "Spirit". Perhaps you pray "Come,
Holy Spirit", or you remember the poem of St. John
of the Cross:

How gently and lovingly
you wake in my heart,
where in secret You dwell alone;
and in Your sweet breathing,
filled with good and glory,
how tenderly You swell my heart with love.[3]

Your little breath is drawn into the great breathing that travels through the universe. "The whole earth is full of his glory" (Is 6:3). You are also full of his glory. This prayer in which you are filled with light and love becomes unavoidably praise and thanksgiving. You become conscious of the *good,* loving power that is the life in all life; which penetrates everything and does not let itself be limited by time and space.

But it is important that you do not influence your breathing, that you do not begin to take deeper breaths in order to get more of the Holy Spirit! The Spirit is God's *gift.* If you try to capture him, take hold of him, he disappears. Every effort here is useless. Let your breathing be itself. Just be still; conscious that your capacity is greater than you imagined in the beginning. Then your breathing can deepen little by little, and you grow into ever greater harmony with the great Breathing . . . "It is the Spirit himself bearing witness with our spirit that we are children of God" (Rom 8:16).

[3] Saint John of the Cross, *The Living Flame of Love*, stanza 4, in *Collected Works of Saint John of the Cross*, 640.

Holy Repetition

You can also repeat a holy word. We know that Jesus
prayed in this way in the garden of Gethsemane, with
"the same words" (Mt 26:44, Mk 14:39). The author
of the *Cloud of Unknowing* recommends that we use
only one word, and preferably a single-syllable word.
(God, love . . .).[4] I personally use two words, for example; "Abba! Father!" Jesus prayed in just this way
in Gethsemane: "Abba, Father" (Mk 14:36). According to Saint Paul, it is these very words that the Spirit
prays in us (Gal 4:6). In another place, he says that
we "have received the spirit of sonship. When we cry,
'Abba! Father!'. . ." (Rom 8:15). Our cry is a share in
the Spirit's cry.

You do nothing more than merely repeat "Abba! Father!" In this repetition, you flow together with the
Son, in the Holy Spirit, toward the Father. You are a
son in the Son, a child in the Child. You do what he
does and has done from all eternity. You acknowledge
that you are the Father's child. You "exercise" your
sonship. In the eternal exchange of words "Father"—
"My beloved Son", the mystery of everything is revealed. You sum up mankind's response when you ut-
ter your "Abba! Father!" before him. Naturally, you
are often distracted. As soon as you notice this, you

[4] *The Cloud of Unknowing*, trans. William Johnston (Garden
City, N.Y.: Image Doubleday, 1973), 56.

return to "Abba! Father!" You have something concrete to go back to. The *Cloud* speaks about "this
work". But at the same time, this "work" is so simple
that it does not disturb your rest; on the contrary, it
leads you into an ever deeper rest.

From my own experience and that of others, I have
learned that it can be an advantage in the beginning
not to think of one's breathing when repeating this
prayer. But when you have dedicated a longer period
of time to this prayer, it can happen that you suddenly
notice that you are actually praying in rhythm with
your breathing, that you say "Abba" while breathing
in and "Father" while breathing out. The prayer has
integrated itself with your breathing without any effort on your part. That is why I use a "two-word"
prayer: it easily finds its place in the rhythm of one's
breathing.

Of the three "ways" I have described, the last, the
prayer of repetition, is in my opinion the simplest and
surest. With the prayer of relaxation and the prayer of
breathing, there can be a certain risk, at least for those
for whom God has not become living and real, so that
one "becomes fixed" in the body, so to speak. Relaxation can, for example, remain merely a psychological
practice, where surrender stays in the background. In
the prayer of repetition, there is not this risk. Here
everything is direct prayer, assuming, of course that
one does not merely repeat the word mechanically but
truly has the basic intention of "streaming" toward the
Father via the word.

Every prayer is a stepladder toward eternity, since in prayer we always seek contact with God. But when we pray for "things", we do not always reach our goal. We remain perhaps on the lowest rung of the ladder and think more of our own advantage than of God. Contemplative prayer, on the other hand, is like an arrow that flies directly to God. And it arrives.

Time continues to pass, but, in the midst of time, you experience something of eternity. You listen to eternity that murmurs within you. It is no longer "painful" to be a creature limited by time. Time is no longer divided into three dimensions that hunt and chase each other. You do not feel tormented by the constant passing of time. No, time stands still. Everything is concentrated in the present moment, and the present moment is endlessly rich and many-faceted. It is not a static position, as when one suddenly stops a film. The present, the eternal now, which we can already reach through prayer here in time, is communion with him "who is and who was and who is to come" (Rev 1:4, 8).

6

Stop!

In contemplative prayer, time is not merely time. Time is filled with eternity.

But it cannot be the intention that after our prayers we will immediately leave eternity and fall back into a time that rushes past. If we are creatures of eternity, we cannot content ourselves with living one half-hour or an hour a day in eternity. For a Christian, time and eternity always belong together. We have our home in God (Eph 2:19).

Prayer and Work

When we rise from our prayer, it means, not that we "finish" it, but that we let it flow out into our work. We take with us something of prayer's rest when we move on to our daily occupations. Prayer is something we really and consciously *begin* but that we never truly finish.

By this, I do not mean that during work time we should turn a part of our attention to God and another part to what we are doing. Such a division in our attention is a heavy load on the nerves and creates fatigue. Many novices in contemplative Orders have become over-strained and high-strung because they tried to live consciously in God's presence at all times. There is a great deal of work that does not leave room for thinking about God and perhaps speaking with him but that demands our total attention. We have seen that Christian time coincides with our mission. God gives us time because he gives us a mission. He gives us exactly the time needed in order to carry out our mission. If we are attentive and can wait patiently, he also gives the inspiration and guidance we need just at the right moment. When we can say with Jesus: "It is consummated", we die and leave time.

You live in Christian time—a time that is filled with eternity—when you consider and carry out your work as a mission from God. When you work solely because God gives you this to do just now, you live simultaneously in time and eternity. Outwardly and from a superficial point of view, you devote yourself to different things that all take "time". But on a deeper level, this variety of things becomes one, because all of them are elements of your mission. You clean, write, teach, eat, sleep, but fundamentally you always do the same thing. And when someone asks "what are you doing?", the answer is always: "I am saying Yes to God, I am the handmaid of the Lord."

Your occupations, however many and varied they may be, flow together into one great task, because you meet them with one single, unchanging basic attitude

—*obedience.* This word is not popular today. But can we perhaps rediscover the liberating reality it contains?

The one who works out of "obedience" lives in a wonderful freedom. He does not need to be afraid that the result is not gratifying, that there will not be enough time, that others will not be content. He is free from all such considerations that make man into a slave. He does his work like a child who plays before the Father's face. As Carmelites, we learn in the novitiate to deny ourselves the satisfaction of completing a work in order instead to be ready to go when the bell rings. One is finished with as much as God wills that we do, and that is true satisfaction.

This continual obedience is not given to us from the beginning. It requires systematic practice in order to grow into it little by little. During prayer you are defenselessly surrendered to God. There you allow yourself to be created by him; there you are permeated with his serene, eternal now. There you can also learn to see everything with his eyes. Immediately after prayer, it is still easy to live and work in this climate of eternity. Something of the incense still lingers from prayer.

But after a while, you slide imperceptibly into stress again. You look at the clock and think that it is going too slowly, your face and shoulders become tense, *you wish to be absolutely finished.* You lose contact more and more with the inner Master. You no longer work to "do his word" (Ps 103:20), but instead you are again a slave during work time. The work rhythm is escalated, which means, not that you "do" more, but that you use and probably waste more energy.

A Fork in the Road

When you become conscious of this, you stand before a fork in the road. You can let this process go its way, lose even more of your inner substance, and let yourself be tyrannized by work, or you can check yourself and say: Stop!

We know this little word from traffic. We come across it regularly. It is also easy for us to accept and obey it there. To ignore the stop sign defiantly would imperil our own life and the lives of others, not to mention the hundred dollar bills that we would rather not get rid of. But when it comes to winning or losing our "soul", the duty to stop is more difficult.

As soon as you notice that something is not right in your way of working, that you become tense and stressed, that you do not work in a spirit of surrender and with anxiety, it is time to respond and say: Stop! Before you continue your work, you return to the proper inner disposition. You can close your eyes and let your hands rest on your lap for a few moments and quietly place yourself in the wave length of eternity again. "Whom have I in heaven but you?" (Ps 73: 25).

Because you are a unity of spirit and matter, soul and body, you can also take note of how your body behaves during work time. Particularly for those who are not yet sensitive enough to register their inner attitude, the body can function as a barometer. Why do you sit with your shoulders raised and tense; why the deep wrinkles on your forehead; why do you hold the pen so tightly? "Let go!" You do not need to be so intense when you write.

Perhaps your poor back that is so painful is telling you it is time to say "Stop!" and correct your external and thereby also your internal disposition. Your back does not feel good when you sit so slouched. Straighten up your spine, and let it be in harmony with the inner disposition you desire. An uplifted heart does not go well with a hunched back.

We must learn not to throw ourselves headlong into work but, instead, begin with a little "Stop!" We can take the time to assume the right disposition, to renounce all egocentric motives, and open ourselves to God's will and power. Before we begin to work, we can make the sign of the cross over our work and call down a blessing upon it. We can pray for all the people who will in some way be affected by our work. It is important at least to *begin* well.

Archbishop Bloom's Little Exercise

There is a great risk that little by little we will lose the right disposition again and return to the old bad habits. But we can, of course, *begin again*!

In his book *Beginning to Pray*, Anthony Bloom recommends a little practice that is worth its weight in gold.[1] I have practiced it often myself and experienced its blessings. The exercise consists in stopping time when things are moving full speed, when you are in the midst of great activity and in a hurry. For many of us, this hurry is almost the normal situation. You are about to do something you consider important, something that gives you a feeling that the whole world is at stake. And you say: "Stop!"

If you have the courage to do this, you will discover something essential. You will notice, Bloom says, that the world does not collapse. We often deceive ourselves and imagine that duty, love for our neighbor, our health, and our career force us to complete this work. It may be true, of course, and a little common sense is good to have. But often it is not so. The work can wait. If I am by chance lazy and slow on a certain day, the work must wait much longer than it does during the brief pause this practice requires.

You say to yourself, for example: "Whatever happens, I will finish in an hour." The simplest way to do this is to use a timer. You wind it up and decide: "Now I will work without looking at the clock until it rings."

To look constantly at the clock is one of the bad habits of our time that prevents us from living in the present moment. You read the present moment on the clock. In reality, you do not look at the clock because you are interested in the present moment; you do so

[1] Anthony Bloom, *Beginning to Pray* (Mahwah, N.J.: Paulist Press, 1970), 85–87.

because you live in the future. The clock shows how much time you have left to finish your work, how many hours remain before you can leave the office, how much longer you must sit and listen to a boring teacher. This constant "clock watching" indicates that you are fleeing from the present moment, from God. Eternity does not wait for you "somewhere else", but precisely here and now. You can meet God only if you rest in the reality that is right now.

Courses in practical psychology sometimes recommend competing with the clock in order to work more effectively and quickly. You say to yourself: "I will read this chapter of twenty-six pages in half an hour." You take your chronometer and begin! For someone who is lazy by nature, it can be healthy to push oneself to an active effort. But as a general disposition or fixed rule, it is disastrous: one cultivates systematic haste. Such advice is typical for a culture that thinks only of performance and results but has no sense of interior growth and maturity. It was an immense liberation for me when one day I removed the clock from my desk and placed it behind me.

There is a harmonious rhythm and continuity in time that come from God and where everything is allowed to develop at its own pace. If we constantly try to manipulate that rhythm, we disturb God's creation and bring chaos where he wants to bring order and peace.

This is no easy practice. If I write a letter or prepare a sermon, perhaps an interesting thought comes to mind in that moment which should be reserved for God. It seems absolutely reasonable to jot it down first before I take a break. But no, it is a question of not giving in. Experience shows that this interesting thought does not disappear. And often, if I dare to lay it aside to remain in God's stillness, it comes back to me more developed and formed. Or also, other, better thoughts come instead. After five minutes of rest in God's peaceful presence, I can now work with greater attention and concentration. Hurry and haste block our creative powers. Peace and calm, on the other hand, release their inner source.

In the monastery, we receive "stop signs" every day, namely, when the bell rings for the Divine Office or meals. But nowadays, out in the world, everyone has a telephone, but, instead of considering it a nuisance, we can let it serve as a stop sign. It gives us a chance to interrupt suddenly the work in which we were perhaps about to drown and be completely available to the person who needs us.

These interruptions can be immensely taxing, but they can be extremely healthy, if we take them in the right spirit. We have an opportunity to take some distance from work, to slow down the speed, to set ourselves free from the tyranny of work. Perhaps we do not have time for everything we had hoped to accomplish, but that can be excellent. To experience continually having our plans thwarted is frustrating for the old man within us but liberating for the new.

I admit, there can be too much of a good thing.

When you feel the irritation rising, and you are soon about to explode, it is wise to "pull the plug" and allow yourself a proper break. One should never force oneself to practice an exercise that exceeds one's capacities.

You do not need to have scruples and feel that you are neglecting your duty when you stop every hour and devote five minutes to allow time to be re-filled with eternity. An English study at a factory showed that introducing a five-minute break every hour, which reduced the work time by 7 percent, had the effect of increasing production by 30 percent. Realizing that our work can be become even more effective by this, we would be wise to say: "Stop!"

These short pauses in our work have the same purpose as the day of rest (sabbath) at the end of the week. We become conscious that time does not exist primarily to produce but to open ourselves to God's eternity and to rest in it. "Let us therefore strive to enter that rest" (Heb 4:11).

7

I Do Not Have Time

There is an almost infallible sign that we do not live in synchronization with God's time. Namely, stress. As soon as we become stressed, we lose contact with reality's deep dimension. Stress draws us to the surface. Stress causes God no longer to be a part of the picture; it causes us no longer to see *all* of reality.

There Is Always Enough Time

According to the dictionary, to be stressed is to live under straining conditions marked by a lack of time. Just this impression of a lack of time indicates stress and is the direct opposite of an attitude that is characterized by trust and surrender.

Most of us have a lot to do. But we can never have *too* much to do. There is always time for what we have to do. When God gives us a mission, he also creates the time needed for it. If there is no time for it, then it is not a task that comes from him but, rather, a work that we have arbitrarily taken upon ourselves, a job that falls outside of his plan for our life.

This principle naturally presupposes an obedience to

God's will in our *whole* life. We must not hastily draw the conclusion: "Aha, then God does not want this", when we think there is not enough time. Perhaps the solution is, instead, that we correct other elements in our life, for example, by abstaining from something that really causes us to "waste" time. There can never be a lack of time. "I glorified you on earth," says Jesus, "having accomplished the work which you gave me to do" (Jn 17:4). If we are tormented by the feeling that there is never enough time, it is perhaps because we try to complete a work that the Father has *not* given us to carry out.

Even at the workplace, we usually have our pet illusions. We think we have so much, so much to do. But rather often, it is our own ambition and not at all a concern for God's glory and kingdom that drives us in our work. It would be a sign of wisdom if we often asked ourselves the question: "Why do I really want to do this?", and then answered as honestly as possible. If we could always say like Jesus: "I do not seek my own glory" (Jn 8:50)! But maybe we must take this reproach of his as meant for ourselves: you "who receive glory from one another and do not seek the glory that comes from the only God" (Jn 5:44).

By what speed ecumenism would advance, for example, if everyone who worked in the service of their respective churches sought only the glory of God and did only the work God gave them to do!

When we feel stressed, our first task is to examine if

we have really received this particular work as a commission from God. If we can claim with certainty that God wills it, we should not, for that reason, believe that everything is in order. It is not merely a question of *what* we do, but also and primarily about *how* we do it. What we have to learn is a new *way* of working, a new way that is characterized by peace and calm instead of stress.

How do we get there? I will point out two ways.

Exchange Fear with Trust

There is always an element of *fear* in stress. We are afraid of failure, of not having the energy, that we will not be finished, of not being accepted.

Fear is conquered by *trust, surrender.* God never tires of repeating for us that we need not be afraid. Exegetes have counted that this is said 366 times in the Bible. If we would look up all these passages, we would have a text for every day of the year, even in a leap year!

We are not alone. God is with us. "I am not alone," says Jesus, "for the Father is with me" (Jn 16:32). All our fear comes from the fact that we are separated from God or, rather, that we *think* we are separated from him. This illusion of isolation makes us powerless.

Is it strange that we have a feeling that our work always exceeds our capacity when we try to do alone what was intended to be done with God? Yes, not only with him—it is he who wants to perform the work through us. Our mission is to be his instrument. "O LORD, you will ordain peace for us, you have wrought for us all our works" (Is 26:12). It is a source of deep peace to know that God always wants to be and always is the *causa prima* (the first cause) and that it is enough for us to be the *causa secunda* (the second, subordinate cause).

"You will not reach it by hurrying, Rufinus, but by worship", said Saint Francis (1181–1226) to one of his companions. "The LORD will fight for you, and you have only to be still" (Ex 14:14). A stillness, a peace, and a calm immediately come when we *know* that it is the Lord who is fighting for us.

Our lack of trust results in acting tensely, and this very stressful attitude blocks us. "If a person is not able to get hold of a thing, he should remain completely still, then the thing will take hold of him", says the German mystic Heinrich Suso (ca. 1295–1366).

I read in the Swedish newspaper (*Svenska Dagbladet*) about a psychologist who thought he had discovered laws of nature that he had not learned in school, two laws that are perhaps two sides of the same coin. (1) We do not have any chance of reaching what we strive for until we give up completely. (2) What we wish most of all to avoid is what we are moving directly toward.

There is a lot of truth in that. As long as you *desire* to become a saint by your own strength, straining yourself and believing you are on the way there and have almost arrived, the decisive breakthrough cannot happen. Only when you have laid the whole thing in God's hands and said to him "You may do as you will" is there a chance that you will step over the threshold, if you also really let him do as he wills.

"Every inner storm, every dissatisfaction, always comes from the fact that one wishes to do something himself", says Eckhart (ca. 1260–1327). But you can be more sensitive to the inner restlessness, fear, and dissatisfaction. Each time it can be a pointed finger: "Trust more in him!" "Commit your way to the LORD; trust in him, and he will act" (Ps 37:5).

We have the power to make an inner movement by which we let go of ourselves, our worry, our stubbornness, or whatever it is that holds us captive. A movement that is not at all complicated but that only demands *the courage* to leave ourselves. We can be rather sure that our obstinate disposition will return after a while, but it is nevertheless an extremely important step in our growth every time we make this movement. We can practice until we have greater facility in this. No one else can do it for us; only we ourselves can let go of ourselves. But there is a trick to finding the way: that we notice where in our body our obstinacy in the present concrete situation is located, and then relax in that place. It becomes a trampoline to an inner freedom.

Only God can bring about the final liberation, but he does it only if we have prepared ourselves.

The Good Self-Confidence

Self-confidence and trust in God are not opposites of each other, as we may sometimes think. It is truly not wrong to have self-confidence. The more you trust in God, the more self-confidence you have. Then you know that God wants to work through you, that he wants to dissolve your resistance, to release your powers. It is not that God sets your gifts and abilities aside when he begins to act in and through you. Instead, he makes them reach their maximum capacity.

Your gifts were created to be activated and inspired by God. "Apart from me you can do nothing" (Jn 15:5). Your violin reaches its maximum capacity when it is God who is playing it. But in any case, it is the violin that makes the sound.

God and man are not competitors. God never wishes to place man in the shadow. He wants to draw him into the light. To trust in God does not mean, then, that you may no longer trust in yourself. Just now, you *may* begin to trust in yourself, in your true self. Just now you can begin to discover your real power. When you live in communion with God, you become invincible. Trust in God makes you great, not small. If God were a foreign power working in you, your role would be reduced to that of a passive spectator. But God works *through* you, not in you. He makes *you* work in a way that far surpasses your normal abilities.

But the requirement for truly reaching your highest

capacity remains always this, that you no longer seek your own advantage. The first step toward the true, permanent self-confidence is that we understand that self-denial, practiced in our own concrete situation, is the very thing that leads us to become who we really are. "Whoever loses his life for my sake will find it" (Mt 16:25).

If we lack self-confidence, it is perhaps, in the end, because we do not believe that God will work, give, love . . . *through* us. We believe that we are not usable instruments. And if we believe this, we become, in fact, useless. Then we are obliged to resort to our own superficial, limited power, or rather powerlessness. Then we lose sight of our own real strength, that which we find in our center, where God dwells. A God who is more "I", and who up until now we considered to be our I, a God who says continuously, "All that is mine is yours" (Lk 15:31).

This applies if we truly *believe* that we are useless, that we have no place to fill, and thereby do not allow God to use us. A *feeling* of inferiority is, on the other hand, not dangerous in itself. It can depend on so many different factors, (our background, psychological mood swings, the influence of others) and can be a cross we must bear. But, at the same time, we can constantly deepen our faith and trust, so that what we are capable of doing has an indispensable place in God's kingdom. Then we can carry out courageously, day by day, just what we have received as a mission and defy all conflicting feelings, not in order to bask in our excellence, but in order to love everything and everyone.

We need not be afraid of fear! In the measure we are aware of our fear, we also perceive our abilities. It is enough to leave our isolation and renew our contact with God.

Discover Your Rhythm

Rhythm is defined as change between stronger and weaker moments that create a regular pattern. Everything that is living is characterized by rhythm. Each person has his own rhythm. The rhythm of one is quicker than that of another. There are few things that are so decisive and typical of a person than simply his rhythm. And at the same time, few things are so overlooked.

Much misery comes from not respecting our rhythm. You cannot be yourself if you force yourself or are forced by others to follow a rhythm that is foreign to you. Constantly violating one's natural rhythm leads to an inner chaos. In the end, one loses one's sensitivity to his own rhythm and no longer has the ability to make a judgment if a certain work or way of working is suitable for his physical or psychological capabilities. One is no longer "in form", that is, in one's right form.

"Things come and go in a deeper rhythm, and people must be taught to listen; it is the most important thing we have to learn in this life", writes the

Dutch Jewish woman, Etty Hillesum (1914–1943), in the camp for transport to Auschwitz.[1]

It is difficult to remain in contact with God when we do not take our own rhythm into consideration. Our personal rhythm is a concrete expression of God's will. We do not live in his will when we live faster or slower than the rhythm he has intended for us.

What incites us to nervousness or panic is never God's will! It is our own illusion that makes us believe that we must absolutely do certain things within a certain time. "For everything there is a season" (Eccles 3:1). What do we do with this ancient wisdom? Could we not develop a sensitivity for our own rhythm, have a reverential respect for it, have the courage to speak one's mind when someone or something wants to trample on it? If we are not in harmony with our rhythm, we are not in harmony with God.

It means that we do not look anxiously to the right or to the left to see what others are doing, how much they produce or do. It is not the rhythm of another that we should take as the norm, but our own. Each one of us has the right to be himself, to follow his rhythm. The one with a quicker rhythm can learn to wait for the one with a slower rhythm, and the slower can stop competing with the quicker. When each one is in harmony with himself, then there is a harmony that is formed within the group.

---

[1] *Etty Hillesum: An Interrupted Life, the Diaries, 1941–1943, and Letters from Westerbork* (New York: Henry Holt, 1996), 332.

It can naturally happen that circumstances force us to follow a tempo that we do not think suits us at all according to our first spontaneous reaction. But our rhythm is not absolutely fixed. There are unsuspected possibilities of adaptation within us in order to carry out harmoniously and calmly what seems to be impossible. We need much sound judgment in order to be able to decide when we may expect the surroundings to adjust to our rhythm or when we should adjust ourselves to the rhythm of our surroundings.

A criterion: Play. How does one know that he has found his own, personal rhythm? There is a clear criterion. Work loses its weight and becomes almost play. If one is usually completely exhausted in the evening, if work is experienced as a heavy burden, it is evident that he has not found his own rhythm.

If one obeys one's rhythm, work becomes a joy. Typing is a splendid example. If I type too quickly, I will inevitably make many mistakes, which becomes a source of increasing irritation. Since the mistake must be corrected, in reality it goes more slowly than if I were not in a hurry. If, on the other hand, I type slowly, at the pace of my own natural rhythm, the keyboard becomes almost like a musical instrument. The typing is less tiring and goes faster. It becomes a game with the keys. It can go so far that it even seems as if the keyboard were producing the thoughts. The text writes itself.

Not everyone types, but everyone walks. *How* do we walk? It can be a delight to walk. We can also run nervously or drag ourselves along. If we find the right rhythm, walking becomes almost a dance. And we should actually always live in such a way that we are in harmony with the cosmic dance that modern science increasingly believes is to be found in the universe.

The right rhythm both presupposes and creates relaxation. The tension or relaxation of the body is a reflection of an inner attitude. If we wish to develop our sensitivity for the right rhythm, there is hardly a more direct way than relaxation exercises. Tensions indicate a wrong rhythm. Relaxation exercises teach us to register our tensions and thus make us attentive to the fact that we are not living according to our rhythm.

Not everything is going to be easy. Pain and difficulties belong to the condition of our earthly life. But if we allow God to be there by respecting our rhythm, it is inevitable that play will have a place in our life. Then we can be relaxed in our depths in the midst of difficulties. And the tears become an integrated part of the universal game that life is.

8

Holy Forgetfulness—A Holy Memory

Memory is a two-edged sword. Without memory, I would never have a real identity. I would not recognize myself to be the same person today as I was yesterday. How could I be faithful if I did not remember my vow? How could we meet each other if we did not remember our agreement? And what good would our meetings be, how could they lead to deep, lasting relationships, if we did not recognize each other? Without memory, the world would be chaos.

But the memory also has something treacherous about it. The memory distorts reality. To meet a friend of one's youth after a separation of many years can be a bitter disappointment. I thought I would meet a happy, open person again, but the one I actually meet is not like my old picture. He is blasé and has lost his faith in life. And inversely, how difficult it is to meet someone without bias when I "remember that he once hurt me terribly".

Actually, I should not then blame my memory but myself, who used it in the wrong way. The memory, like everything else in the world, can be used and misused. Instead of understanding that the picture I have in my mind corresponds to something that was real before but is no longer, I have the tendency to force what I remember of the past onto the present reality. I see, not reality, but a worn-out image. I am striking windmills that were torn down long ago.

I can never live in reality if I do not learn to tame my memory. The memory tends to be overactive. It presents images to me in season and out of season. If I do not wish to be caught off guard by all of this material, I must learn to sort it all out. Some of it is useful, but much of it is rubbish. Sometimes it is good to remember, but often it is better to forget.

Learn to Forget

We can hardly find a more competent teacher in this art than Saint John of the Cross. His radicalism intimidates many, but those who wish to go the whole way and reach the top of the mountain in this life often return to him. Here we find someone who is totally consistent!

If the most important thing in life is to "love the Lord your God with all your heart, and with all your soul, and with all your mind, and with all your strength" (Mk 12:30), it is obvious that we must not let the powers of our soul go their own way. Everything in us is intended to converge and be directed toward one single goal, God. All our powers should be invested in loving him. Therein lies our vocation, and therein also lies our unity. We are created to be directed "one way", toward God. To give ourselves to what distances us from God or does not lead to him is to waste time and miss the purpose of life.

Applied to our memory, it means that much of what we usually remember may be forgotten. In his famous *Cautelas* (*Precautions*), Saint John of the Cross writes: "Never be scandalized or astonished at anything you happen to see or learn of, endeavoring to preserve your soul in forgetfulness of all that."[1] In his *Counsels to a Religious on How to Reach Perfection*, we read "Whether you eat, or drink, or speak, or converse with lay people, or do anything else, *you should always do so with the desire for God and with your heart fixed on Him. . . . And in forgetfulness of all the things* that are and happen in this short and miserable life."[2]

In his *Sayings of Light and Love*, there are many passages that treat of just this theme. For example: "Be interiorly detached from all things and do not seek pleasure in any temporal thing, and *your soul will concentrate on goods you do not know.*"[3] "Leave as well all

---

[1] Saint John of the Cross, *The Precautions*, no. 8, in *The Collected Works of Saint John of the Cross*, trans. Kieran Kavanaugh, O.C.D., and Otilio Rodriguez, O.C.D. (Washington, D.C.: ICS Publications, 1991), 721.

[2] Saint John of the Cross, *Counsels to a Religious on How to Reach Perfection*, no. 9, in *Collected Works of Saint John of the Cross*, 728 (emphasis added).

[3] Saint John of the Cross, *The Sayings of Light and Love*, no. 96, in *Collected Works of Saint John of the Cross*, 92 (emphasis added).

these other things and attend to one thing alone that brings all these with it (namely, holy solitude . . .), and persevere there *in forgetfulness of all things.*"[4]

We can object, and with good reason, that all of these texts are written for his brothers in the Carmelite Order, that is, to people who have expressly chosen a contemplative life and who have resolutely directed their existence, even in its external form, to prayer and contemplation. In a Carmelite monastery, one may forget a great deal that one is forced to think about when living outside the monastery. This would include, for example, everything to do with money and what one may, with a good conscience, forget when one has taken a vow of poverty. But in every monastery there is also a bursar, and he gives perhaps more time to "unrighteous mammon" (Lk 16:9) than the average person. Still, even he is a Carmelite, and Saint John of the Cross' rules apply to him, also.

The asceticism of the memory for which Saint John of the Cross is asking, however hard it may seem, is in essence extremely flexible and actually suits everyone. Assuming that one lives in God's will and may consider his work as an assignment from God, all the thoughts and memories that are necessary to carry out this work are actually "directed toward God". There can be no conflict between God's will and God.

Saint John gives clear answers to those who would gladly take their longing for prayer as a pretext to ne-

[4] Ibid., no. 79, p. 91 (emphasis added).

glect their work: "Thus people are not required to stop recalling and thinking about what they must do and know."[5]

The rule for the asceticism of the memory is in practice: Remember what you ought to remember in order to do what you have to do; beyond that, you may live in a holy forgetfulness. No one can claim that this rule is too hard or too absolute in his situation. Consideration for the situation is built into the rule itself.

No One Needs to Go Beyond His State in Life

Saint John of the Cross' ascetical rules mark out a path, show a direction. No one can fulfill them immediately —just as no one can immediately fulfill the first commandment: to love God with one's *whole* heart. Saint John of the Cross speaks to people whose hearts are already enkindled with love for God, for whom God has become real.[6] When God has become a magnet, it is easy to forget everything that is not him.

It is then experienced, not as something one *must* do, but as something one is *allowed* to do. What a relief to be free of everything that previously made life so small and narrow and finally to be allowed to live in God's boundless immensity! Afterward, one notices that "the holy forgetfulness" becomes more and more God's work. It is he himself who leads the

[5] Saint John of the Cross, *The Ascent of Mount Carmel*, bk. 3, chap. 15, no. 1, in *Collected Works of Saint John of the Cross*, 290.

[6] Ibid., bk. 1, chap. 14, no. 2, p. 151.

person into forgetfulness by drawing him to himself. "When united with God . . . its imagination being lost in great forgetfulness without the remembrance of anything is absorbed in a supreme good."[7] Also, when it is a question of work, one notices that God begins to take over the responsibility. It is he himself who activates the memory when one needs to remember something. One receives a more tangible proof that he himself holds the helm and that one may trust him. And the more one trusts him, the more active he is. One is drawn into a "good" cycle.

We could make a paraphrase of the above quote from Saint John of the Cross and say: The memory, when it is united with God, is totally present in everything, remembers everything, recalls everything, because then it sees and registers the real truth in everything, and there is no reason to forget that. Then one rests in the remembrance of the great whole, and the small details, of themselves, so to speak, appear at the right time and in the right place.

One need not be very advanced before one can surrender the helm.[8] It is not to saints but to completely ordinary people that Jesus says: "Do not be anxious about your life, what you shall eat or what you shall

[7] Ibid., bk. 3, chap. 2, no. 4, p. 269.

[8] Wilfrid Stinissen, *Into Your Hands, Father*, trans. Sister Clare Marie, O.C.D. (San Francisco: Ignatius Press, 2011), 91; Stinissen, *Inre Vandring* (Stockholm: Libris Förlag, 1999), 156; Stinissen, *Natten är mitt ljus* (1985; Tägarp Glumslöv: Karmeliterna, 2016), 97–98.

drink, nor about your body, what you shall put on. . . .
Look at the birds of the air. . . . Consider the lilies of
the field, how they grow" (Mt 6:25–26, 28).

A Risky Asceticism?

Is it not dangerous to practice this asceticism of the
memory? Do we not already forget more than is necessary, we who do not remember where we have left
our glasses and our keys? Does the memory not become dulled when it is constantly quieted?

No, there is no risk here of early senility! To "forget" does not mean that mental pictures fade away
and in the end completely disappear but, rather, that
one does not call them to mind. The explanation is
simple. According to Saint John of the Cross, mental images are stored, not in the memory itself, but in
another faculty, namely, the imagination (*la fantasia*).[9]
To forget them is nothing more than to leave the images stored up in the imagination in peace. They are
available whenever one needs them.

Besides, we all know that when we cannot find our
keys, it does not depend on a weak memory but on the
fact that we were not really "present" when we left
them in the car. If we had been living in the "present
moment" when we stepped out of the car, instead of
being occupied with our "memories", we would not
have any difficulty "remembering" what happened to

[9] Saint John of the Cross, *Ascent of Mount Carmel*, bk. 3, chap.
13, no. 7, p. 288.

the keys. When it comes to a poor memory, a great deal of our complaints depend on a faulty impression: all too often, we act automatically, without being really awake.

The ability to recall images to mind, on the other hand, is never so active and alert as with the one who tries to live according to what Saint John of the Cross prescribes. If one forgets all non-essentials, it is only to create space consciously for another memory: that one is in God's hand, loved by him, created for him. That is the mental image one prioritizes and untiringly "reminds" oneself of. Such a resolute activity definitely does not lead to a poor memory.

I say "resolute activity". If one simply allows the mental images to surface without sorting and prioritizing, we end up in chaos.

All religions, all philosophers are in agreement about this. But we Christians also know that to the same degree that we empty our memory of everything that is irrelevant, we open ourselves to receive not only something, but Someone.

To live in what *was* closes the door to what *is*. Nothing new can happen with the one who clings to the old. "Throughout my whole life," writes Paul Claudel (1868–1955), "I have tried to live toward what is ahead and to free myself from melancholy and sorrow over what has been, which does not lead to anything other than to weaken one's character and imagination."[10]

---

[10] Quoted in A. M. Carré, *Chaque jour je commence* (Paris: Cerf, 1977), 11.

Old, repressed sorrow must be allowed to come up to the conscious level, and here psychotherapy can play a positive role. But licking old wounds is not the best way to cure them. Old sorrow should be neither cultivated nor directly combated. Transformation of the past happens primarily by openness to what is new in the present moment.

Do Not Forget What God Has Done (Ps 103:2)

Holy forgetfulness does not exclude a holy remembrance. As I have already suggested at the beginning of this chapter, our memory is an asset. It is thanks to our memory that we can learn something from history. The tragedy of Auschwitz can make mankind wiser, but only if we do not allow it to sink into an "unholy" forgetfulness.

The memory connects us to the past, present, and future. Everything that was, and to a certain degree even what is to come, can become present in the now by memory. Detached events receive a context, and what seemed to be completely scattered finds a unity. Thanks to memory, I can glance over my life and find a hidden meaning. Yes, according to Boethius (ca. 480–524), eternity is: "to have everlasting life completely and fully in one's possession".[11] Then we may say that memory can give us a little taste of eternity.

The memory can create discord by drawing us out of the present moment and causing us to live in an

---

[11] *Interminabilis vitae tota simul et perfecta possession.*

unreal past, but it can also create *unity* by giving us the opportunity to draw the past into the present and so give us a comprehensive view of our life.

We can only have a true, comprehensive overview if we try to see our life with God's own eyes, if our memory, to a certain degree, coincides with God's "eternal years".[12] God sees that our whole life is "his handiwork". With the help of our memory, we can go through our life and see how everything that happened to us was or has been transformed into grace.

Our memory tells us that God has thought of us, worked with us. Such a memory pours itself out in praise: "Blessed be the LORD, for he has wondrously shown me his merciful love" (Ps 31:21). Each one can, in his own way, say with Mary: "He who is mighty has done great things for me, and holy is his name" (Lk 1:49).

Saint John of the Cross, who so earnestly exhorts us to forgetfulness, even when it is a question of extraordinary graces from God (for example, visions and revelations), gladly accepts our "recalling" these moments of grace *if* it is not in order to experience the same wonderful feelings as the first time but in order to enkindle our love for God.[13]

The distinction can seem subtle, but it is neverthe-

---

[12] *The Living Flame of Love*, stanza 2, no. 34, in *Collected Works of Saint John of the Cross*, 671.

[13] Saint John of the Cross, *Ascent of Mount Carmel*, bk. 3, chap. 13, no. 6, p. 288.

less fundamental. It tells me if I am seeking myself or God; if I am led by egoism or love. The only important thing in life is to grow in love. "When [the] evening [of life] comes, you will be examined in love."[14] Love is the ultimate criterion.

There are even, according to Saint John of the Cross —and now he is equally eager in his praise of "the holy memory" as he previously was in praise of "the holy forgetfulness"—graces that are impressed like a seal on the soul, so that they remain long and often never leave the soul. "This is consequently a great grace, for those on whom God bestows it possess within themselves a mine of blessings."[15] The memory gives us access to a gold mine. How we use the gold depends on us. We can invest it in "self-realization" or in love and praise. The choice is ours.

The Maturation of the Memory

It is interesting to see how the memory can develop and mature.

When I read the psalm verse "forget not all his benefits" (Ps 103:2), I think first of all of some obvious "blessings" that have marked my life: that I had such wonderful parents whose deep faith brought me into the Church; that I was called to Carmel; that Jesus

[14] Saint John of the Cross, *Sayings of Light and Love*, no. 60, p. 90.
[15] Saint John of the Cross, *Ascent of Mount Carmel*, bk. 3, chap. 13, no. 6, p. 288.

Christ wanted me as his priest. But gradually, the circle of blessings widens. My gratitude is no longer awakened by some individual outstanding events. I notice that an even greater area of my life bears the imprint of God's loving care. What the Psalmist says about the earth, I can say about my life: it is "full of the mercy of the LORD" (Ps 33:5). The Lord has carried me on his wings my whole life (Deut 32:11). Everything I remember gives witness to his love.

The risk of ending up in sterile daydreams becomes ever less. One does not get fixed primarily on the external event in what is remembered now but, rather, on the word of love that God has spoken and speaks through it. All memories lead to gratitude.

If you are aging, perhaps mental images from the past surface in greater measure than when you found yourself at life's biological peak. There is no reason that it would be different for you than for most people. As a Christian, you are an ordinary person. But what can be an escape for others and an unhealthy waste of time becomes for you a prayer. If previously you possibly got tired of the constant repetition of "his mercy endures forever" in Psalm 136, now it is this very verse that best expresses your inner disposition. Your memory turns your entire life into a song of praise.

If we claim with Saint Thérèse of Lisieux that "everything is a grace", we cannot exclude our sins. Saint Teresa of Avila adds, after having described the lukewarmness and laxity that characterized a part of her monastery life: "[I have] shown such excessive ingratitude."[16] "But even from this. . . . Your infinite goodness has drawn out something worth-while; and the greater the evil, the more resplendent the wonder of Your mercies."[17]

Saint John of the Cross stresses that God does not annihilate the sin but, rather, transforms it. In the *Spiritual Canticle*, he lets the soul sing:

> Do not despise me;
> for if, before, you found me dark,
> now truly you can look at me
> since you have looked
> and left in me grace and beauty.
>
> (Stanza 33, 2)

And he comments "Since you have looked (rubbed out this dark and wretched color of sin that made me unsightly)".[18] He quotes the Bride in the Song of Songs who is conscious of being both black and beautiful (1:5). "That is, now I can indeed be seen, and I merit being seen by receiving more grace from your eyes. The first time you not only rubbed out the dark color with those eyes, but you made me worthy to be seen since you looked with love."[19] If the bride should forget that she has been black, she would minimize her

[16] Saint Teresa of Avila, *The Book of Her Life*, chap. 14, no. 10, in *The Collected Works of Saint Teresa of Avila*, vol. 1 (Washington, D.C.: ICS Publications, 1976), 101.

[17] Ibid.

[18] Saint John of the Cross, *The Spiritual Canticle*, stanza 33, no. 6, in *Collected Works of Saint John of the Cross*, 603.

[19] Ibid., stanza 33, no. 6, p. 603.

bridegroom's love and the transforming power in his eyes.

Even here, it is a question of seeing with God's eyes. He no longer sees any evil; he has forgiven. He sees only the fruit of his love.

"Do This in Memory of Me"

In the sacraments of the Church, we have access to a completely special form of "holy memory". One could say that in the sacraments, the memory is so concentrated, so condensed, that it is not only images that we recall but *reality*. The actual reality of the past becomes present, fresh and new in the now.

The sacraments are an effective antidote to our unfortunate tendency to flee from the reality of the moment by means of the memory and to live in the unreality of times long ago. In the sacraments, it is not we who return in our thoughts to events of days gone by, but these events come to us themselves as actual reality. In the sacraments of the Church, and only there, "remembrance" and reality coincide.

Every sacrament is a "commemoration" of a certain aspect or episode in Jesus' life on earth, a commemoration that makes us see the eternal dimension, so that in just this aspect or action Jesus becomes contemporary with us.

In a person who is baptized, Christ becomes present in his death and Resurrection. The person dies to the old, sinful life and exchanges it for a new life. But it can only happen because Christ draws him into his own passover from death to life. It is always *with Christ* that he is buried and raised up (cf. Col 2:12).

When I go to confession and confess my sins to a priest of the Church, Christ is present in me, he who once and for all confessed the sins of mankind on the Cross and by his Resurrection showed that the Father bestowed "absolution" (forgiveness) on him. The cosmic confession of Jesus on the Cross has an eternal dimension. That is why it can be present and real in every person who confesses his sins. At the same time, he is present in the priest who pronounces his own words: "Your sins are forgiven."

When two young people get married and have their covenant of love blessed by the Church, Christ comes to them, he who himself *is* the New Covenant of love. Every marriage is an image of the unique marriage between Christ and the Church (Eph 5:31–32). More than that, every marriage *actualizes* the original marriage of Christ with the Church, and it is only because an individual marriage is integrated into Christ's all-embracing marriage that it can last. God not only wishes to give spouses his blessing and help them remain faithful to each other; in Christ, God himself is the great covenant partner who draws the person into his own love and faithfulness.

But it is above all in the Eucharist that the "holy memory" is fully realized. When the priest repeats Jesus' words "Do this in memory of me", the word "memory" receives an extremely powerful and charged meaning. Now it is no longer one or another aspect of Jesus' life that becomes present, but his entire life is present here and now. On the Cross, Jesus has concentrated everything he has been and done during his life. It is this concentration, this total offering of himself in love, that is the actual reality every time we celebrate the Eucharist.

This sacrament is a grandiose victory over the crushing power of time. In the Eucharistic commemoration, the Eternal gives himself to us, not as raised above or detached from time, but as most deeply involved in time. In his death and Resurrection, which is the central point of history, he tears down the barrier (Eph 2:14), and the barrier between the past, present, and future as well. Everything is present simultaneously. And this total presence comes to us when we do "this" in memory of him.

In the prayer "O sacrum convivium", Saint Thomas Aquinas sharply and concisely gives expression to the Eucharist's power to transcend all borders. Here the present, the past, and the future are one:

> O sacred Banquet in which Christ is received.
> The memory of his Passion is recalled
> The Mind is filled with grace
> And a Pledge of future Glory is given to us.[20]

---

[20] "O sacrum convivium", original Latin (punctuation from *Liber Usualis*):

> O sacrum convivium!
> in quo Christus sumitur:
> recolitur memoria passionis eius:
> mens impletur gratia:
> et futurae gloriae nobis pignus datur.
> Alleluia.

9

To Redeem Time

Saint Paul speaks twice of the importance of "redeeming" time. In a more literal translation, he writes to the Ephesians: "making the most of the time, because the days are evil" (5:16). And in the letter to the Colossians we find it in a corresponding way: "Conduct yourselves wisely toward outsiders, making the most of the time" (4:5). The original Greek text has *exagorazomenoi ton kairon*. And the Vulgate translates it: "redimentes tempus". *Exagorazō* means first of all "to redeem", so Saint Paul also writes: "Christ redeemed (*exēgorazen*) us from the curse of the law" (Gal 3:13). *Exagorazō ton kairon* is a standard expression that means: make use of the time or opportunity. "Make good use of time", says the 1981 (Swedish) translation. This is surely what Saint Paul means. One must not waste time. It is precious and limited. It is precisely by using time well, by "making the most" of it, that one redeems it.

According to Saint Paul, everything created has fallen under the dominion of futility (Rom 8:20), even time. It is our task to liberate it from its bondage to decay (Rom 8:21), to make the time of sin into a holy time. Every time we refuse to place time at the service of egoism and, instead, allow it to follow the ways of love, we contribute to the liberation of time and transform it into an eternal, incorruptible time. Love is itself eternal, and, in the presence of love, "corruption" has no possibility of lasting.

The Tyranny of the Past

We can think also of our past here. It is precisely in relation to our past that we experience bondage most strongly. Our past can freeze to ice in us. Then we carry it with us as a heavy burden. It has been described as "the tyranny of the past".[1] We can seem to be pursued by our past.

If we did not receive enough love as children, if we had too strict an upbringing, if we were constantly criticized by our parents, we carry with us a feeling of not being good for anything. Our past has us in its grip. Is this not what characterizes neurosis: that one gets fixed in the past? Neurotics cannot leave the old and live in the now. They are slaves to what has been.

Perhaps it has not been so bad. Maybe we had wonderful parents who poured out their love on us. But we have nevertheless reacted in our own way to life's many challenges. We have learned to master the situation, to deal with certain strains. We have done it in a certain way, which can easily become a pattern, precisely for the reason that it proved adequate previously.

[1] Lennart Lundmark, *Tidens gång och tidens värde* (Stockholm: Författarförlaget Fischer & Rye, 1989), 149–52.

It invites us or even presses us to react in the same way when similar circumstances occur. These old reaction patterns restrict our freedom. Instead of meeting the situation with an open spirit, detached and unbiased, the response is already fixed. In principle, nothing new happens any longer. Unconsciously, we do as we have always done, and thereby we block the ever-flowing life stream that wants at every moment to create our life anew.

The old, egocentric man has a peculiar understanding of time. For him, it is almost only the past that has value. He cannot see the future as anything other than a repetition of the past or, in the best cases, as a battle against it. But even the one who fights with his past invests energy in what *was* instead of taking advantage of the possibilities *now*. It is always the present moment that feels the pinch. For the old man, the present moment lacks meaning. The present is nothing other than a quick, insignificant transition from the past to the future. The present has no value in itself. It serves only as a kind of means of transportation that moves the past to the future.

When I identify with my ego, I see my fellowman through glasses that are colored by what I have already experienced in my previous contacts with him. If he has hurt me, I expect that he will hurt me again. I am on my guard and spread out my prickly thorns. Then I complain because he has not been friendly to me this time, either. But how could his friendliness reach me when I hide behind my defenses? Or else

I have only good memories of my former encounters with him and expect him to show me friendliness this time, also. If he is then, by chance, a little distant or depressed, I become depressed. He is not the same as he was before, and I experience that as an offense.

If I live in this way, my past becomes a tyranny that forbids me to meet people as they are. I become completely incapable of seeing them in their reality and truth. The only thing I meet is the image I have created of them. Instead of meeting a living person, I meet a lifeless image. It is no wonder, then, that we have difficulties really reaching out to each other.

The Gospel exhorts us to leave the past. When a man comes to Jesus and declares that he will follow him wherever he goes, the answer is: "Foxes have holes, and birds of the air have nests; but the Son of man has nowhere to lay his head" (Lk 9:58). Everything that made up his security before, everything that had been taken for granted over the years, having a fixed dwelling place and a sheltering home, all of this is an obstacle when it comes to following the Master.

To another who wishes first to go and bury his father, Jesus answers: "Leave the dead to bury their own dead; but as for you, go and proclaim the kingdom of God" (Lk 9:60). Why do you tarry over what is dead? Turn toward life!

To a third, Jesus says: "No one who puts his hand to the plow and looks back is fit for the kingdom of

God" (Lk 9:62). One cannot begin something new when he remains fixed on the old.

Can we do anything better for our neighbor than to free him from the fetters of the past? It was Jesus' mission to proclaim liberty to the captives. Everyone who wishes to follow him is invited first to become free in order then to be able to liberate others with him.

Transform Your Past

One does not free oneself from the tyranny of the past by repressing old experiences. Repression never solves any problems. What has been repressed continues to haunt in a hidden corner of the unconscious and lead to inexplicable anguish, aggression, or melancholy.

Rather than letting yourself be tyrannized by your past, you can be the one who guides it yourself and thus make something beautiful out of it. You turn your old way of being and doing upside down. Instead of letting the present and the future be a repetition of old experiences, you take your past in your hands and give it a new meaning out of the present. It is the present that decides what the past means. There are unlimited possibilities before us here.

Even if the past is in a certain sense gone, it is nevertheless not inaccessible. You have access to it not only thanks to your memories; it is also material that waits to be worked on. What your past means depends on what you do with it now. As long as you live, no event is completely finished, nor is it gone. It is your task to "redeem" the past, to infuse new life into it continually.

A person decides himself if his past is a heavy burden that he drags along with him and makes him act in a stereotypical and compulsive way or if it is an asset. What happened in our earlier life is not made of granite. It is more like dough that we can knead and to which we can constantly give new form. It is an extremely exciting work to let what seemed to be deprived of all meaning become meaningful. As a spiritual director, I have the privilege of witnessing this life-giving process with many people.

It would be crass materialism to believe that what has happened is unalterable and fixed. The event as a fact, naturally, cannot change or be undone. But the substance of the event is not its factual reality but its spiritual content, its meaning. And this is always open to change and development.

Thus, the past is not something that only binds; it also invites us to constantly new, free attitudes. If something in our past life feels heavy or meaningless, that can be taken as a signal, as encouragement to set to work with it. One of the finest things about man's freedom is that it allows him to decide what meaning his past will have. He does not have complete control over the external course of events, but he can freely decide what the events mean for him.

If in our day we so often question the concept of

man's freedom, it is generally because we become fixed on factual reality and do not understand that what is essential in what happens is its meaning. It is typical for a spiritually mature person to be less dependent on the external situation. He has a wondrous ability to let everything that happens become valuable and meaningful.

God is secretly present in everything that happens. Not a sparrow falls to the ground without him being there (Mt 10:29). Not a single moment of our past has escaped him, and, in his sovereign omnipotence, he inserts everything into his plan to perfect his work. The more we live in communion with him, the more we can realize and unite ourselves to his designs, which transform all factual occurrences into stones for building the "new city" into which the world is being transformed by him.

Forgiveness

A basic requirement for being able to redeem time is to *forgive* and to let oneself be *forgiven*. It is above all our feelings of guilt that hold us in the grip of the past.

There is no person who does not sometimes make "wrong" decisions. Instead of taking care of your aging mother yourself, which she urgently asked you to do, you leave her at a home for the elderly, where she is tormented by loneliness and sorrow. After her death, you constantly remember anew her pleading voice, her reproachful look. And now, it is too late . . . Your guilt feelings weigh on you, but "there is nothing you can do about it."

But yes, there is something you can do about it. To the degree that it is a question of real guilt, you can lay it before God's loving gaze. As soon as something is placed there and is exposed to the radiance of his love, it is taken up into the light and becomes light itself. No guilt can resist God's forgiving love. It is a tremendous liberation when you concretely, in your inmost self, dare to take a leap of trust and believe that God *really* forgives and that you *may* let go of your guilt feelings. Anyone who has experienced this can bear witness to what kind of new creation it entails.

If it is not a question of real guilt but, rather, of unwarranted guilt feelings, it is important to see this clearly. The truth sets us free. To the degree that a guilt feeling is revealed as groundless, it releases its strangling grip. If it does not do that, the reason probably lies somewhere else, perhaps in another, real, unforgiven guilt.

Guilt feelings have a paralyzing effect on time. Time, which has been given to us so that we might grow and mature, loses its dynamic power when we live in guilt feelings. They can suck out all the strength of time like leeches.

Guilt feelings can have their origin in one's own guilt, but they can also stem from the fact that we have still not chosen or been able to forgive others the injustice they have done to us. For many, it is a question of forgiving their parents. However well-meaning parents have been, they have often been unable to avoid causing a certain amount of pain to their children, because their own wounds, which, in turn, were perhaps caused by their own parents, were not healed. This is original sin seen most concretely.

Not to forgive them their "fault" means that we remain in the old injustice they may have caused us. We refuse to finish that chapter and therefore never move farther in the book of our life. It seems easier to lay the guilt on our parents than to take responsibility for our own lives. But in principle, it is more difficult. To stand and stomp our feet in the same place makes life monotonous and joyless.

Many believe that they cannot forgive. But we can do more than we think. We can at least begin to desire to be able to forgive and to pray for this. It is unbelievable what miracles can happen when we finally take hold of ourselves and decide to "go farther". A disciple of Jesus is called to "go on [his] way today and tomorrow and the day following" (Lk 13:33).

It is easier to forgive others when we have exposed ourselves to God's forgiveness. We pass on what we have received. If we live in God's love, we spread this light. Our deepest problem however, is that we find it so difficult to believe in God's forgiveness. We project onto God our own unwillingness to forgive. But to forgive is never a problem for God. It is his nature. He would not be who he is if he refused to forgive.

If we read the Bible, it ought always to be because we desire to meet Love, to go deeper into it and be more convinced of it. The Bible is a dangerous book if we get stuck on individual passages and do not understand that, as a whole, it is one great declaration of love from God. There is one leitmotif in the Bible: "The Father himself loves you" (Jn 16:27), or also "For God so loved the world that he gave his only-begotten Son. . . . God sent the Son into the world, not to condemn the world, but that the world might be saved through him" (Jn 3:16–17). All the other passages must be interpreted from this leitmotif.

There is much in the Old Testament that can lead us astray if we do not interpret it from the New Testament —for example (Deut 32:35), "Vengeance is mine, and recompense." If we stay with these words, we can easily begin to believe that God is seeking revenge. But the meaning is not that God will take revenge, but that *we* may not seek revenge, since retribution belongs to God. Saint Paul has understood it in this way: "Beloved, never avenge yourselves, but leave it to the wrath of God; for it is written, 'Vengeance is mine'" (Rom 12:19). We know that God's wrath is a wrath of love and that he gets revenge by an *excess* of love.

Forgiveness is master over time. The blockage that sin has brought about is shattered by God at the first opportunity and becomes the beginning of a new development. Time that was imprisoned and stood still is set free and becomes a flowing force again.

> Where thou art not, man has naught,
> Nothing good in deed or thought,
>   Nothing free from taint of ill.

Heal our wounds, our strength renew;
On our dryness pour thy dew;
    Wash the stains of guilt away.[2]

Forgiveness turns the time of tyranny into a time of hope. If I constantly stand in the rain of God's forgiveness, I am continually washed clean and renewed, and then I can also forgive others and myself. Why would I not forgive myself, when I know that God forgives me?

A New Creation

"God knows all", writes Saint Ambrose (ca. 340–397), "but he waits to hear your voice, not in order to punish, but to forgive" (*non ut puniat sed ut ignoscat*). *Ignoscere* originally means: not to know. When God forgives, he does not see sin in the first moment in order to forgive in the next moment. The moment God hears the sinner's voice placing his sin before him, forgiveness is also there. God does not have a chance to see the sin, so to speak. He sees his own mercy. We can truly speak of a simultaneous interpretation. But in contrast to the current simultaneous interpretation, this simultaneousness is absolute. Under God's gaze, sin is immediately dissolved in his mercy. Forgiveness is not just to wipe out or forget. God's forgiveness —and even ours, in the measure we take God as an

[2] Sequence from Pentecost, *The Roman Missal*, Revised Standard Version, 2nd Catholic Edition, vol. 1 (San Francisco: Ignatius Press, 2012), 445.

example (Eph 5:1)—is a new creation. God creates anew and transforms the past. That time that appeared to be irrevocably lost, "imprisoned", is redeemed by God. And thereby our thanksgiving is also set free. It now becomes possible "always and everywhere" to thank God. God is Lord of time. He can even bless "retroactively". What a help in the struggle to let go of all sorrow over what cannot be undone and of things undone that can no longer be done!

> The time is out of joint: O cursed spite,
> That ever I was born to set it right![3]

Is it not rather the reverse? How happy I am since I am born with the ability to "tame" time!

While psychoanalysis often presents the past as a great villain that is responsible for my complexes, faith sees the creative power that lies hidden in the failures of traumatic experiences of the past. Sin, that of others and my own, can become grace; failure can contribute to greater trust; loneliness can lead to a deeper encounter with God. A real understanding of Christian time can perhaps be had when one has had the opportunity of doing wrong and discovered that it does not necessarily block development but can, rather, hasten it.

[3] Shakespeare, *Hamlet*, act 1, scene 5.

All Time Is Already Redeemed in Christ

It can seem rather hopeless when we become aware of our task to "redeem" time. Is it not a mission that exceeds our ability? Especially since, when it is a question of the past—and it is this we have focused on here—there will always be a great deal that remains unconscious and that therefore cannot be consciously "redeemed", either.

There is much in our life that is enveloped in darkness and that will remain dark as long as we live on this earth.

But this is not a problem! *All* time has been redeemed, once and for all, by Jesus Christ. In him, everything is concentrated (Eph 1:10). He is the Alpha and the Omega, he who is and who was and who is to come, the Almighty (Rev 1:8). That which was and is to come is gathered together in him in a constant, transparent, and radiant now.

Just as he has transformed all suffering into love by taking upon himself all suffering out of love, so he has also transformed everything that is dark and meaningless in our past into light by taking mankind's time and destiny upon himself. There is no wound, no trauma that has not already died and been resurrected with Christ. In him everything is transfigured once and for all. We may trust in this ultimate transfiguration. We may rest in it.

Mankind's memory is concentrated in Christ. He has bestowed this memory on the Church through the Holy Spirit. "The Counselor . . . will teach you all things, and bring to your remembrance all that I have said to you" (Jn 14:26). With his help, we can decipher and "redeem" our past. It does not matter if we do not have time to decipher everything before we die. The Spirit "searches everything" (1 Cor 2:10), and he has been given to us (Rom 5:5).

10

Fidelity

We have spoken of the past and how we can transform it: not by thinking or brooding over it constantly —there is much we may forget—but by making something beautiful *now* out of the material that our past offers us. The destiny of our past is decided in the present.

And the future? Do we have any control over it?

We can make plans for the future and in that way try to direct it, but at any moment, something can occur that annihilates all our plans. You want to become a doctor, but halfway through your studies, you begin to suffer from an incurable disease. Instead of a doctor, you become a patient, perhaps for the rest of your life.

We can never get a firm grip on the future. It eludes both our judgment and our authority. The more plans, the greater the risk of disappointment. And is it not written that we should not be troubled about the future, that it will take care of its own troubles (Mt 6:34)?

Still, it is possible for man to take up his entire future in the present moment and give it direction. He can make an irrevocable decision, make a final vow and remain faithful to his vow. The one who is faithful to the vows he has made masters the future. The future is no longer a horse that runs away. Fidelity tames the horse and lets it gallop toward a determined goal.

Fidelity Versus Spontaneity?

Do we not feel divided before the concept of fidelity? On the one hand, we long for faithfulness. If faithfulness is lacking, we cannot trust in each other; then there is no security in our relationships. Love itself becomes a torment when I know that at any moment I can be abandoned. The adjective that the word "friend" evokes most is "fidelity". Without fidelity, there is no real love.

But, on the other hand, we are more than ever allergic to anything that comes close to coercion. We want to be ourselves and not be forced to pretend a love that is no longer there. Would it not be dishonest to want to be "faithful" at all costs when I feel that my love is dead? Do I not have the right to change? Must I force myself to live according to a decision of days gone by when today I am another person? And what is that love worth which is not spontaneous? Is my friend really deserving of an "obligatory" love? Perhaps it offends him more than if I should abandon him. Can one command love to exist? Is it not the essence of love that it is spontaneous?

According to my dictionary, something is "spontaneous" when it occurs by a sudden impulse and is not built on forethought; and a person is called "spontaneous" when he acts according to his feelings. If one demands that love be "spontaneous" in this sense, one does away with faithful love definitively. Feelings are typically changeable, that is, not "faithful". If a man chooses a woman, or a woman lets herself be chosen, only because she is beautiful or attractive, the relationship is doomed to failure in the long run. It is as good as certain that the man will meet women who are more beautiful and attractive and thereby awaken stronger feelings. Faithfulness has no chance if love must be absolutely spontaneous.

But there is a deeper "spontaneity" that does not follow the pace of our impassioned and subsiding feelings. Man does not consist only of changing feelings. There are deeper levels in him. It is the *will* that is love's real organ. The only love that is worth the name is the love that *wills* the good of the other.

Just as there are superficial and deep feelings, so there is also a superficial will and a deep will. These two wills are opposed to each other. The superficial will stands in the service of egoism. It *strives to save its life*. The deep will assents to or even coincides with man's original, genuine being that was created to give itself in love. Deep within every human being lies sleeping the knowledge that one can save one's life only by losing it, that one finds himself by forgetting himself, that there is no freedom as long as he remains fixed in the prison of his own small desires and superficial feelings.

It is on this deep level of the will that "spontaneity" can really blossom. It is there that I am truly myself.

What is born out of this ground level belongs totally to my true essence. It gives me a feeling of reality, genuine life. It wells up out of my true nature and is therefore "natural" in the right sense of the word. Here there is no place for desperate effort and, thus, no risk that spontaneity will be lost.

When Saint Augustine says "love and do what you will", he does not mean it is enough to fall in love in order to come into the land of freedom. Genuine love is only possible from the depths of one's being, where one *is* love. What grows on the tree that has its roots in our depths can never be bad. It can only be the good fruits of love.

Man Can Choose

When I took my final exams before graduation, our class was told to write an essay on the following subject: "*Few people follow their vocation. It is easier to let oneself be directed by life than to direct oneself.*" At that time, "Humanities" still made up an important part of education. The high school years were aimed not only at attaining knowledge but also at becoming a better person. And it was the purpose of the essay to elaborate on the fact that to be human included the ability to make decisions, to will something with one's life, to decide for oneself the direction of one's future. One believed in freedom, and by freedom was understood a person's freedom to choose between different alternatives, to decide which to engage in, and thereby also to direct his future.

However obvious that sounds, there are, in our day, many who no longer believe it in practice or in theory. While determinism seems to be heading toward a sure death in science, it continues to live a tenacious, insidious existence in the way many people think, feel, and act. I don't have the energy to swim against the stream, one sighs, and what is the advantage of doing so anyway? Things will be as they are. The general weariness and feeling of meaninglessness that fill the atmosphere in our time lead to a kind of paralysis. Freedom is considered by many to be an illusion.

Others do not deny freedom, but they give it a peculiar definition. For them, choosing is just a way of restricting freedom. To choose is, of course, always to exclude something else, and the more radical the choice, the more possibilities that are excluded. To choose a spouse for life means that all other potential spouses are excluded. Every choice is thought to make life narrower and to make us less "free" to choose later without hindrance what we feel like. We think that we preserve our freedom by not choosing. All possibilities remain open when one refrains from taking a position.

With such a concept of freedom, it is difficult to make a decision. We have not understood that a little bit of true freedom means more than unlimited possibilities. What are possibilities worth if they are never realized?

With religious people, this inability to make decisions sometimes has a pious exterior. We wish to remain open to God and let ourselves be led by the Spirit who blows where he wills at every moment. We do not know today what the Spirit will say tomorrow. Would it not be wrong to restrict God by making irrevocable decisions? Rather than fixing the future and leading it in determined paths, we wish to live in the present and, moment by moment, respond freely to the Spirit's impulses.

It sounds very nice. Actually, too nice. Such an excessive spirituality denies the principle that grace builds on nature. It is part of man's nature to have a life's project and engage himself in it. Certainly, it *can* happen that God's Spirit may inspire us to begin something totally new, but, as a rule, he gives his inspirations within the framework of the form of life we have once and for all decided to follow.

Moreover, it is unrealistic to believe that from the beginning we have at our disposal such fine antennae that we are in a position to perceive and interpret the Spirit's movements at every moment. Instead, there is a great risk that we confuse the guidance of the Holy Spirit with our own desires. Most of us need a longer time of systematic practice where we consciously "renounce" our momentary desires and impulses and allow ourselves to be led by our reason. We should not despise the light of reason as though it were less than the guidance of the Holy Spirit. Reason is an integral part of his guidance. He directs us to a great degree by the understanding of our reason. And reason tells us that we do not accomplish anything in life if we do not make long-term decisions.

Faithfulness or "Steadfastness?"

Many of us are certainly in agreement that a promise or vow should be kept. To break a vow without scruples is still considered a betrayal that undermines mutual trust. What is rather in question is if it is wise to make long-term vows. Is it wise to force the future to flow in a river bed that I have dug once and for all? Do I not force myself to live a life that is ruled by *duty?* It is, of course, my *duty* to remain faithful to what I once decided. But is it not the same as killing life? Life is supposed to be movement, development, change.

No, duty is not in itself something dead. If it is performed with the heart and not only mechanically and statically, it becomes a lasting instrument in the service of faithfulness, and if faithfulness sometimes does not really have the energy to "follow along", duty can be its "vicar".

The French existentialist Gabriel Marcel (1889–1973) points out that faithfulness (*fidelité*) is something different from steadfastness. "Steadfastness" is when one stands by what he has chosen, a consistency that, according to the dictionary, does not yield or give way. Steadfastness is almost synonymous with perseverance. One perseveres in the same position or situation without letting oneself be disturbed. The word steadfastness makes us think of unchangeableness.

I can assure my friend that my attitude toward him has not changed; that I have the same feelings as I had on the day our friendship was born. And perhaps I do exactly as I have always done: I write for Christmas and his birthday. I let him know when I have moved to a new address. I call him when something important happens in my life. My proof of friendship reaches him with the punctuality of a clock. A more "steadfast" friend one could hardly imagine. But when he is in need; when he goes through a long depression; he does not hear from me. It is not a part of the routine I had originally envisioned.

"You are those who have continued with me in my trials", says Jesus (Lk 22:28). If I leave my friend alone at his most difficult time, if I am not *with* him during his "trials", can I then call myself a friend? Friendship is reduced to certain unwritten rules that I have once and for all determined. I consider myself faithful when I keep these rules. But can *he* experience me as faithful?

Such a steadfastness has very little to do with love. It is perhaps, rather, a product of self-love. One does not wish to appear unfaithful or deceptive. That kind of "faithfulness" shown in friendship is concerned, not with the friend's distress and need, but with one's own ambition to be correct and irreproachable.

Even in relation to God, we can exchange faithfulness for steadfastness. I entered the Carmelite Order in my youth in order to live for God in the most radical way possible. If my life consisted of being "faithful" to my radicalism as I understood it during my novitiate, it could hardly be called life.

Life is growth. I may not content myself now with giving to God what I gave of myself in the beginning of my monastic life. God constantly points to new zones in my being, whose existence I did not even realize when I was young. He wants me to allow him to enter in there, also. To love God is much more radical than I realized when I began. The love to which he invites me is always greater. Faithfulness to my vocation is, above all, faithfulness to the One who calls me, and I can always come to know him more and more.

The risk to which one is exposed in a human relationship is also there in one's relationship with God: the risk of placing oneself on a certain level and allowing "faithfulness" to consist in a constant repetition of the same words, the same prayers, the same small acts of self-denial.

I have given a description here similar to Gabriel Marcel's of a constancy or steadfastness that is cold and that has its roots in a carefully disguised egoism. But there is naturally also a good constancy that is indispensable for loving faithfulness to blossom.

Faithfulness has its seat in the heart, but constancy is more of a rational adherence to that to which my heart wants to remain indissolubly faithful. If one's reason acts without communion with the heart, its fruits are hard and dead. But if reason, and in this case well-informed constancy, stands in the service of the heart, it becomes a *help* and a *support* for the deepest aspirations of the heart, which are not always so easy to realize under the conditions of this life on earth.

Creative Fidelity

In genuine fidelity, one does not mechanically repeat old patterns or walk in habitual paths. True fidelity has a creative power.

It is similar to God's creative power. At first sight, it can seem as though God, when he has once created, only contents himself with repeating what he has done. Perhaps we do not believe even this. Our spontaneous impression is that God's act of creating is something that only happened in the beginning. Later, when creation is "finished" (Gen 2:2), it appears to go its own way and manage on its own. In reality, God is constantly creating anew. His "fidelity" to creation shows itself in that he makes it new every moment. There is no dawn that is just like another, nor any sunset. Meteorologists' greatest puzzle is that the weather forecast is seldom correct. However much data is collected, the result of the data still does not correspond with reality.

If we only understood that to turn our constant hunger toward "something new" in the right direction, we would be satisfied to overflowing, both in the kingdom of nature and in that of grace. To "tire" of something is impossible for the one who lives with God. God's faithful love makes it so that everything he creates—visible and invisible—is filled with new life at every moment.

Nature is more flexible in this respect than man. It *lets* itself be created and is therefore always fresh and new. Man, however, resists being created. He would rather create himself, and the result is an everlasting repetition of old clichés.

True fidelity has creative power. There is no limit to its inventiveness. It knows nothing of routine. Even if the same words and expressions are used—vocabulary is, in any case, limited—they constantly receive new power from the inner flame. In principle, it is not even important to find new words or ways of acting. "It is the Spirit that gives life" (Jn 6:63). You can pray the surrender prayer of Charles de Foucauld (1858–1916) every day, and every day pray it in a new way. Yes, it is possible that you experience how it grows in you or you in it, so that you pray it from an ever more genuine expression of what you want and are.

> The familiar path
> never grows old
> if our eyes are filled with light.[1]

[1] Birger Norman, Swedish journalist, poet, and novelist (1914–1995).—Trans.

If fidelity were a matter of holding fast to certain rules or behavioral patterns, it would condemn us to being unfruitful. But fidelity always has to do with love. Fidelity is to affirm constantly the love one once promised another person or God. Since love is life itself, fidelity promotes life. Stagnation is unthinkable. Fidelity breaks through all borders; it always finds a way beyond what we originally had in our thoughts when we made our vows or promises.

Fidelity belongs to the essence of love as the body belongs to man's person. That is why Søren Kierkegaard (1813–1855) says that fidelity is a valid criterion that makes it possible to place a value on the quality of love. If love comes to an end, it has never been real love.

This claim is perhaps a bit pointed. An "occasional" infidelity, so to speak, does not necessarily prove that the love has not been real. Our human weakness can cause us to make mistakes, but if we open ourselves anew, love lifts us up again. Is there a more beautiful fidelity than the one where we have forgiven one another?

If fidelity would presuppose a pure, completely authentic love, hardly any relationship would last. When love is born, it is, as a rule, a feeble and fragile plant. It demands care in order for it to grow. It comes always as a gift and a task. We receive it as a talent, but we must *care* for it.

However immature love may be when it shyly or vehemently announces itself, most of us nevertheless understand that there lies a great seriousness in it. What ignited the spark was perhaps some temporary qualities, but when the spark is once ignited, it is no longer the qualities one loves, but the other as he is in himself. Characteristics only make up the springboard to something that lies beyond them.

If this is not so, if the whole relationship is built on certain qualities, there is no reason to speak of love. To understand the other as a package of characteristics that one wants to get as much out of as possible is to steal from him. Even the word self-love does not apply here: one does not love himself when he degrades himself by being a thief.

Always

Some people have a natural ease making the leap from characteristics to the heart of the person. Saint Thérèse of Lisieux writes in her autobiography: "God gave me a heart which is so faithful that once it has loved purely it loves always."[2]

The word "always" has a special relevance when it comes to love. To say "I love you" means "I will love you always." Do you not feel you offend the other when you only love him right now?

[2] Saint Thérèse of Lisieux, *Story of a Soul: The Autobiography of Saint Thérèse of Lisieux*, trans. John Clarke, O.C.D., 3rd ed. (Washington, D.C.: ICS Publications, 1996), Manuscript A, chap. 4, pp. 82–83.

When a man and a woman marry, there is an obvious assumption that it is for "all time". One takes it for granted that when a man and woman solemnly bind themselves to each other, it is a final choice. Even in our "liberal" time, divorce is considered a misfortune and a failure. In general, one cannot easily judge those circumstances that lead married people to divorce. In itself, divorce is a betrayal of love "for all time", but for individual cases there are always ways of preserving the heart's fidelity.

That someone is in a position to choose another person "for all time", that is, not because of temporary qualities—those can change or disappear at any time—but because of what the other *is,* shows that he is capable of making definitive decisions. He has power over the future. He can choose for himself the direction in which he wants to guide it. Man can fill the present moment with such a power that it includes both the rest of his life and eternity.

But no one can choose another person and relate to that person as a "you" if he is not himself an "I" who has contact with his center. One can only love another person from the depths of one's being when he transcends time. And the other who is loved in this way receives through this love the help to discover his own depth. Faithful love, which is love that includes the word "always", lifts both the lover and the beloved above time and makes them persons. To be a person is to be able to pronounce the word "always", which transcends ourselves.

Through fidelity, we create ourselves and each other. That is why it is so urgent for young people to awaken the belief that it is possible to make a vow and keep it. It is vitally important to teach them that man is more than a changing psychological development. In his depths, man transcends himself, and it is out of the depths of his being—where God dwells, and where he is God's image—that he can pronounce a vow of lifelong fidelity without knowing how the future will affect his psychological condition. Unfaithfulness is to betray oneself. The one who is unfaithful denies his eternal dimension and becomes a plaything for perishable time.

One may object that circumstances change, that it is impossible to foresee what will happen, that it is therefore unwise to "bind" oneself. But it is really a sign of maturity to maintain one's direction undisturbed in the midst of external changes and in the midst of what perishes to bear fruit that "will abide" (Jn 15:10).

What makes a person a person is not drowning in what happens but, instead, giving everything that happens a meaning and a direction. Even in this, he resembles God: he can use and make use of everything. Everything can be taken up and integrated and directed toward an all-encompassing goal.

To be a person is to be in a position to make a vow and be faithful to it. For most of us, our life's mission consists in fulfilling the vow we made in our youth. Our machines, apparatuses, and computers can make long-term plans that affect not only us but even those who come after us. Should we, for our part, not be able to choose a definite life's direction and stay with it, we who have come to know Love (1 Jn 4:16)?

The Third Party

To promise lifelong fidelity is only possible because man is more than a changing stream of feelings, impressions, thoughts, desires . . . What constitutes him as a person is that he is an image of God, that in his depths he is like him. That is the deepest truth about man.

If we open our Bible, we cannot avoid noticing that what most characterizes God is faithfulness. Israel can abandon God any number of times, but he himself remains faithful. And Israel knows it. How often does it not say: Lord, you are our rock, our fortress, our shield! God makes covenants, and he abides by them, even when his people break their promise. In the end, God establishes a "New Covenant" that is eternally more radical than the old.

On the Cross, he gives himself up to man, and, in the Eucharist, he immortalizes and continuously shows this unconditional love.

To act as an image of God is to try to reproduce something of God's eternal faithfulness. "I will espouse you for ever; . . . I will espouse you in faithfulness" (Hos 2:19–20). I am called to a faithfulness that is like God's. Even if the other person fails, I want to remain faithful. It can happen that I release the other person from the bond that unites us, but I myself do not wish to take anything back. What would the command to love one's enemies mean if it did not exhort me at least to love the one I have promised to love always?

A faithfulness of this kind realizes something of God's love on this earth. It is only possible when God is the third party in the covenant. Therefore, a vow of fidelity that is taken seriously is also always a prayer. Without union with him who dwells within us, and whose image we are called to be, it is presumptuous to promise another person or God love "for all time".

God is the necessary third party in all real love. "Ubi Caritas est vera, Deus ibi est" (Where there is real love, God is there).[3]

In faithful love, man is divinized.

---

[3] Medieval hymn. See *Cecilia: Katolsk Psalmbok* (Stockholm: Veritas Fölag, 1987), no. 568.

11

The Present: Time's Axle

Every time I speak of living in the present—and that has happened often—I notice that people listen with an unusually wakeful and alert attention. It is a subject everyone understands, in which everyone is interested, and about which everyone feels he wants to hear more.

It is also an "ecumenical" subject to the highest degree. Here, all religions converge. One finds the advice to live in the present moment everywhere whenever one is concerned about man's spiritual development. Christ, Buddha, Krishnamurti (1895–1986), and de Caussade (1675–1749) speak of this. All philosophers are in agreement that this is a decisive point. It seems to go with man's original, innate wisdom that he does best when he lives in the present.

Our Exile from the Present Moment

But this deep conviction does not prevent us from systematically fleeing from the present moment. In his Nobel Peace Prize lecture, Octavio Paz spoke of our "exile from the present moment". We have lost the present. It seems we have been banished from the paradise of the now. Often, all that remains with us are painful memories of, to a large extent, past time that has not been spent well and fear of an unknown future.

Perhaps our greatest defect is *absence*. We are always somewhere other than where we ought to be. We come too early or too late. We live in the reality that was or in the one that is coming (though it often does not come in the way we thought it would). We miss reality. "The search for the present is . . . the search for true reality", Octavio Paz also says. Instead of walking in the garden of true reality (paradise), we walk in the imaginary reality of exile, and we are surprised that we are not sufficiently happy! To live in an imaginary reality gives no lasting joy.

To insist stubbornly on following one's own self-chosen rhythm that does not coincide with the real rhythm of time is a revolt against reality and ultimately against God.

All our complaints that we do not have time are actually comical. We lose most of our time by not being present or being occupied when the present moment appeals to us. Jean-Pierre de Caussade describes how it ought to be and can be: "The present moment is the ambassador of God to declare His mandates. The heart listens and pronounces its 'fiat'. . . . It [the soul] never stops but sails with every wind. Any and every direction leads equally to the shore of infinity. Everything is a help to it, and is, without exception, an instrument of sanctity. The one thing necessary can always be found in the present moment."[1]

Time's Axle: The Present

"Which of the three dimensions of time are—in practice—the most important for you?" An interesting question, for which it can be healthy to find an answer. I underline *in practice*. As we know, theories seldom coincide with reality. Does the emphasis in your life lie in the past, or do you live mainly in the future? Or do you belong to the select few for whom the present is central? If so, it remains to be seen what the quality of the "now" is: Is it an all-encompassing now or an empty now?

A Christian is always directed toward eternal life. He seeks "the city which is to come" (Heb 13:14). It seems that concentration on the future is the dominating element in Christian time. But the paradox with Christianity is that the future is fundamentally already the present. The future has shifted to the present. In and with Christ, the kingdom of heaven has come. "The kingdom of God is in your midst" (Lk 17:21). "I really don't see", writes Saint Thérèse of Lisieux, "what I'll have after death that I don't already possess in this life. I shall see God, true; but as far as being in His presence, I am totally there here on earth."[2]

---

[1] Jean-Pierre de Caussade, S.J., *Abandonment to Divine Providence* (San Francisco: Ignatius Press, 2011), sec. X, p. 57.

[2] Saint Thérèse of Lisieux, *Her Last Conversations*, trans. John Clarke, O.C.D. (Washington, D.C.: ICS Publications, 1977), 45.

The eschatological time has already begun. "God . . . made us alive together with Christ", writes Saint Paul, "and raised us up with him, and made us sit with him in the heavenly places in Christ Jesus" (Eph 2: 4–6).

Mystics, the only Christians who are fully "normal", experience this existentially. In deep prayer, we never leave reality but, rather, go ever deeper into what is *now*: in God, in ourselves, in the creation that surrounds us. We imagine deep prayer to be a state where one forgets everything. In one sense, that is correct, but it can also be misinterpreted as though it were a departure from what is here and now. That prayer in which we are ever more united with God is an ever deeper unity with the present moment. There God is present, and everything he has created is living and present. What has been and what is to come stand in a *now* that is transfigured by God. In the deepest prayer of all, it is not a matter of "forgetting all" in order to reach God. We need, not to forget it, but, rather, only to allow it to sink into the present where all problems lose their weight and instead become a "theophany" and an experience of the living God. Everything may be there, so long as we do not allow it to draw us away from the present, which is the only place where we can really meet God.

The present moment is the axle of time. Saint Augustine has no doubts:

It is not properly stated that there are three times, past, present, and future. But perhaps it might properly be said that there are three times, the present of things past, the present of things present, and the present of things future. These three are in the soul, but elsewhere I do not see them: the present of things past is in memory; the present of things present is in intuition; the present of things future is expectation.[3]

The Unique Opportunity of the Present

The present is decisive over our past. We have previously seen how we can give our past a new meaning. Nothing is fixed, everything can be transformed. Everything depends on what we do *now* with our past and how we use it.

In the same way, our future is dependent on the present. It is our life *now* that decides how our future will be. Christianity does not believe in reincarnation. We cannot put off our conversion to a future life. We will have no chances in another life. It is now, in this life, that the outcome is decided.

We can practice our inner receptivity in order to take note of the innumerable opportunities that are offered to us *now* to see what they entail.

The word "today" has a particular weight in the Bible. "You have declared *this day* concerning the LORD that he is your God, . . . and the LORD has declared *this day* concerning you that you are a people for his own possession" (Deut 26:17–18; emphasis added). The Catholic Church sings every morning in its liturgy "O that *today* you would listen to his voice! Harden

---

[3] *Confessions of Saint Augustine*, trans. John K. Ryan, bk. 11, chap. 20, no. 26 (New York: Image Books, 1960), 258.

not your hearts" (Ps 95:7–8, emphasis added; cf. Heb 3:7–8). It is *today*, and not yesterday or tomorrow, that life must be lived.

The New Testament speaks of time with the help of two words: *Chronos* and *kairos*. *Chronos* is neutral time. *Kairos* is the favorable time. *Kairos* is concerned with a particular occasion, an opportunity that God offers to man, a moment when God is very near and lets himself be found.

Ever since God became man and is with us in Jesus "always, to the close of the age" (Mt 28:20), every moment is a chance to encounter him. For a Christian, there is no longer neutral time. *Chronos* in its entirety has been transformed into *kairos*. At any moment, "as long as it is called '*today*'" (Heb 3:13, emphasis added), we can be filled with God.

Martin Buber (1878–1965) tells of Rabbi Mendel from Kotzk that he once surprised some learned men who were his guests with a question: "Where is the dwelling of God?" They laughed: "What a thing to ask! Is not the whole world full of his glory?" But he answered his own question: "God dwells wherever man lets him in." Martin Buber comments: "This is the ultimate purpose: to let God enter. But we can let him in only where we really stand, where we live, where we live a true life."[4]

It is only in the present moment that we can let God enter. Instead, we grieve over not having done it yes-

---

[4] Martin Buber, *The Way of Man, according to the Teaching of Hasidism* (New York: Kensington, 1991), 40–41.

terday, or we also dream of doing it tomorrow. The
real *kairos* is in the present.

The Present Lets Eternity In

The present is the meeting place between man and
God. Outside of the present, we only meet ourselves,
or, more correctly, a counterfeit of ourselves: our dis-
appointments, dreams, and illusions.

The encounter with God in the present occurs in
different ways. God waits for something from us at
every moment, and our task is to respond to his expectations moment by moment. Jesus reproaches the
Pharisees and Sadducees for not being able to interpret
the signs of the times (Mt 16:3), and he weeps over
Jerusalem because the people "did not know the time"
of [their] visitation (Lk 19:41, 44).

We miss God's visitation by doing the wrong thing
at the wrong time; by working when we should be resting, by worrying when we should be giving thanks, by
daydreaming when we should be praying. Even here
it is a question of "there is a time for everything."
"Even the stork in the heavens knows her times; and
the turtledove, swallow, and crane keep the time of
their coming; but my people know not the ordinance
of the LORD. How can you say, 'We are wise, and the
law of the LORD is with us'?" (Jer 8:7–8).

I am wise when I try to rediscover the lost "instinct"
that points at every moment to what shall or shall not
be done. But the most important thing at all times is

to *be* what I really am and not to try to be someone else. In that very moment, I have a completely unique personality that God wills should turn itself to him. That does not mean that I should become comfortable with myself. The true acceptance of myself now entails an openness to God's transforming power that wishes to lead me to the goal where every moment is filled with Christ's life.

The encounter with eternity presupposes this fundamental harmony with God and his will. To live outside of God's will is to live separated from him, and outside of him there is no eternity but only perishable time. But God's will can be carried out in different ways. I can "take it easy"—this is the *thesis*—and try to combine duty and comfort. I am then perhaps essentially on the right path, but the pace is so slow that, considering the shortness of life, there is no chance I will reach the goal before my death. Nor can there be any talk of experiencing eternity in time.

I can also—here comes the *antithesis*—gather all my powers, exert myself to the ultimate extreme, and do everything I can in order to fulfill my mission as quickly as possible. In this I am plagued, not by idleness, but by ambition to run the longest possible stretch in the shortest possible time. Here eternity is still more distant than for the one who "walks" on the road. Here time is a resource of which one always has too little. It passes and passes always too quickly.

But there is a third possibility: *synthesis*. Like the ambitious, I gather all my powers here, but *for a total availability*. I offer myself, my *whole* self, as a flexible instrument to the action of God. The result is not *a work for God*, but *a work of God*. I do not act, but God acts in me (cf. Gal 2:20). Here there is no tension, no real exertion. Nor is there any risk I will become burnt out. Here God decides the tempo. Everything goes according to his own pace, quickly or slowly, but usually more quickly, at least seen on a global scale, than if I were doing the work myself.

We find here again something of the lazy man's freedom from worry, but divested of the sloppiness and nonchalance that characterize his way of acting. Freedom from care is now a consequence of total trust. I discover that the yoke is easier and the burden lighter than I thought (Mt 11:30). Here my action is taken up into God's action *and therefore also marked by eternity*. An eternity that I not only *believe* in but can *experience*.

Something of God's eternal now is reflected in an action that is "given" to him. I am completely in the moment, totally attentive, and totally relaxed. I do not need to be afraid of not being ready. There is someone else who bears the responsibility. I can remain calmly in the present moment, which is eternally narrow when seen horizontally but, at the same time, is endlessly deep when seen vertically, since it stands in harmony with God's eternal now.

One must be a saint, and a great one at that, always to be working in this way and thus constantly experiencing God's eternity in time. Saint John of the Cross writes that: "A soul will hardly be found whose union with God is so continuous that the faculties . . . are always divinely moved."[5]

But all of us who are still not saints can return again and again persistently and untiringly to this selfless attitude or come close to it. Then we will also receive glimpses, and this will happen more and more often, of eternity in the midst of time. The present will become holy because we experience that it is transparent and allows something of God's eternity to come through.

Every Moment Is an Eternity

Someone asked me recently what happened in the Trinity at the Incarnation when God became man. The answer is that the Trinity *opened up for us,* for our participation in their life.

This opening in the Trinity, through which the life within the Trinity becomes accessible to us, is in a particular way tangibly and concretely perceptible in the present moment. It is by living in the present that we participate in the Trinity's eternal now. The present moment is God's garment, his typical attire. Deep prayer that lasts one hour according to clock time can be experienced as a moment, and, inversely, a moment of complete openness to God can have a fragrance of eternity. "Each moment is an *eternity*",

[5] Saint John of the Cross, *The Ascent of Mount Carmel*, bk. 3, chap. 2, no. 16, in *The Collected Works of Saint John of the Cross*, trans. Kieran Kavanaugh, O.C.D., and Otilio Rodriguez, O.C.D. (Washington, D.C.: ICS Publications, 1991), 273.

writes Saint Thérèse of Lisieux to her sister Céline (*chaque instant c'est une éternité*).[6] As is clear from the context, she means that how our eternity will look depends on how we live *now*. Every moment is a building block for eternity. Every moment in our life has consequences for eternity. It is unbelievable what can happen in a moment. "Céline", writes Saint Thérèse one year later, "it seems to me that God has no need of *years* to carry out His work of love in a soul, a ray from His Heart can in one instant make His flower bloom for eternity! . . ."[7] What a consolation for all who are older and grieve over having *wasted* their lives!

But the words "each moment is an eternity" can mean something more. As we saw earlier, the moment is the incarnation of eternity. God's eternal now opens up for us in the moment. The eternal dimension of time is revealed in the present. The condition is that you do not squander your attention on what *was*, *is*, or *shall* be, but that you are completely present in the moment. This total presence, where only the now exists, gives you a sense of eternity. Time stands still.

If we give time regularly to prayer, this experience is probably not foreign to us. When our entire being is recollected in a loving attentiveness to God, or rather

[6] *Letters of Saint Thérèse of Lisieux*, trans. John Clarke, O.C.D., October 15, 1889, vol. 1 (Washington, D.C.: ICS Publications, 1988), 587.

[7] Ibid., October 20, 1890, vol. 2 (Washington, D.C.: ICS Publications, 1988), 714.

when we are pure openness to *his* loving attention to us, then the word *time* loses its meaning. The clock certainly continues to tick, but we are no longer synchronized with it. We live no longer in what perishes but in what will last.

12

Place Yourself Directly
in the Present Moment

Fortunately, eternity is not only accessible in prayer. Whatever you do, presupposing that you respect your conscience and are thus in harmony with God's will here and now, you can conquer the transitoriness of time and experience something of eternity.

Live in Reality!

The only thing required is that you are completely present in *reality now*! Reality coincides with the workings of God. Outside of that, there is no reality. This reality possibly includes the fact that you are suffering, that you are tense, full of anguish. But if you accept the situation in which you find yourself right now, you are in reality, in the center of God's action, and, consequently, in his center. Eternity is opened up.

But do not exchange the acceptance of your present situation for resignation! True acceptance—and this is worth repeating—is an openness to God's transforming power.

God has made the path to him so short and so easy

that we have difficulty finding it. We find ourselves on it all the time. "As soon as you stop traveling you have arrived", writes Thomas Merton (1915–1968) in his journal on March 10, 1947.[1]

In everything that makes up your concrete reality *now*, you encounter God. He does not work in you according to old plans that he made when he began to create you. He continually adjusts to the situation in which you find yourself now, even if that situation is a result of your own lack of faith or sin. If anyone is "realistic", it is God. "The point is that where you are, in the very situation in which you find yourself, he is there, his nearness to you is there and yours to him", writes Hjälmar Ekström (1885–1962).[2] Here and only here and now are you completely one with God.

You do not need to try at all costs to come out of your situation. You can accept it, rest in it, open yourself to your anguish and pain, and meet God right in the center, in the center of your being. Saint John of the Cross says that we can be in our center even if we are not yet in our deepest center.[3] That is a consolation.

Perhaps you are not even capable of this. Then you

[1] Thomas Merton, *The Sign of Jonas* (New York: Harcourt, Brace, 1953), 28.

[2] Hjälmar Ekström, *Den stilla kammaren* (Skellefteå: Artos, 1988), 55.

[3] Saint John of the Cross, *The Living Flame of Love*, stanza 1, no. 12, in *The Collected Works of Saint John of the Cross*, trans. Kieran Kavanaugh, O.C.D., and Otilio Rodriguez, O.C.D. (Washington, D.C.: ICS Publications, 1991), 645.

can rest in your inability to rest and abandon yourself. Even your worry and tension are used by God. "Tension and worry of this kind are not in vain", writes Hjälmar Ekström, "rather, they have their own mysterious mission to carry out, one knows not *how*."[4] God in his wisdom uses everything to lead us to himself. "With everything that happens in our life, with our sin and deficiency, with our sluggishness and foolishness —with everything, he draws us in (into the heavenly world) and we *come* in."[5]

By accepting *what is now* and resting in it, you abandon yourself into the hands of God. At the moment you dare to meet the situation of the moment, you fall directly into God. Then he can use this situation to realize his will and his plan for you, even if the situation is a direct consequence of your sin or that of another. This is surely the secret of the record journey of the saints toward holiness. *Everything* was received as a gift from God, everything gave a hundred percent yield, everything was given back to God in thanksgiving. Every moment led them deeper into him.

If I will not accept, I flee from reality. I slip out of God's hands. Then the situation cannot bear fruit, either for myself or for others. But if I accept, everything becomes fruitful. Every suffering is taken up into Jesus' redemptive work. "All of man's suffering, wherever it may come from, becomes transformed by Him to a bearing of the cross on His way, when he abandons

[4] Ekström, *Den stilla kammaren*, 57.
[5] Ibid., 42.

himself to the Lord. Yes, it becomes transformed into a 'suffering for Christ's sake', even if it should originally spring from another source."[6] The Lord prepares a cross for us out of the suffering if we submissively accept it together with the Giver.[7]

Total Presence

To lay oneself "flat out in the present moment"[8] means to be totally present in what you are doing. *Age quod agis* (Do what you are doing), says an old proverb. When you eat, eat, and preferably do not read the newspaper! When you walk, walk; open all your senses, drink in the beauty of nature, and do not live in your thoughts! When you listen to someone, listen, and do not think about what you will answer. When you sleep, sleep as well as you can, and do not brood over the mistakes of the day that has just passed! Do one thing *after* the other!

Everything has its time. Let there be clear, definite borders between your different occupations. Engage yourself completely in what you are doing now, and leave it completely when you begin something else.

We ought never to have the feeling that we have "much" to do. Right now, we have only *one single thing*

[6] Hjälmar Ekström, *Den fördolda verkstaden* (Lund: Gleerup, 1963; new ed.: Skellefteå: Artos, 1988), 91.

[7] Ibid., 27.

[8] Eva Jagrell, *Omfamnad (dikter)* (Helsingborg: Literaturtjänst, 1984), 31: "Lägg dig raklång i nuet."

to do. We do not need to be troubled about the next moment. It can take care of its own troubles. Every moment has troubles enough of its own (cf. Mt 6:34).

It is presumption always to want to do several things at once. In that respect, we would like to be like God (Gen 3:5). With him there is perfect simultaneousness between the vision and the performance, between the word and the act. "He spoke and it came to be." In the vision you are like God: you can look over your life, its beginning and its goal. You can even have an overview of all history. But when it is a question of carrying out what you have seen, you must go step by step. There you stumble on your limitations, and you harm yourself by not respecting them. What you can do in this moment is so little, and your ambitions are so boundless.

Nevertheless, it is precisely by accepting your limitations and being completely satisfied with the little you can perform in this present moment that you come closest to eternity. To survey the history of mankind in its entirety gives an intellectual satisfaction but no experience of eternity; being totally present in the now does, however. By accepting the clear borders of the moment, not trying to fill it with several things at the same time, the present receives an explosive force that makes it explode into eternity. It begins to resemble God's eternal now. The very least leads to the highest. One thinks spontaneously of Saint John of the Cross' poem "To the Divine":

[I] sank, ah, so low,
that I was so high, so high
that I took the prey.[9]

Total presence means that you are completely engaged in the task of the moment. All your forces are
gathered together. By the fact that all your attention is
directed to one single task, you yourself become *whole*.
Division is conquered. Being present in the now has a
mysterious ability to restore inner harmony, even to release resources that have been untapped until now. The
intensity of attentiveness awakens new powers and allows deeper levels in you to have a share in your work.
By concentrating on the work of the moment, you
yourself become more "centered". You work from
ever deeper levels of your being.

But total presence does not exclude distance. Distance characterizes the typical human way of being.
Without distance, there is no freedom. Total presence
does not mean that we throw ourselves into our work
and allow ourselves to be swallowed up by it. Distance
is an element of respect we show both ourselves and
creation. The right kind of distance enables us to leave
the work at any time. We are not glued to it or pursued by it. Just as there is a clear beginning, there is
also a clearly defined finish. We do not carry with us
any remnant of it that haunts us.

Every step forward in being present means increased

---

[9] Saint John of the Cross, "Otros del mismo a lo divino", no.
6, 3, in *Collected Works of Saint John of the Cross*, 57.

joy and freedom and, above all, increased availability to God and his action.

The right kind of presence almost always goes together with relaxation. What presence is on the psychological and spiritual level, relaxation is on the physical level. What we need is "attention without tension".

The Swedish expression "tense attention" (*spänd uppmärksamhet*) is actually an inner contradiction. What is implied here is that attention is sharpened by being "tense". In reality, attention is hindered by tension. One is cut off from one's deep level by tension. The most important part of the person is not there. The action does not have contact with the source and therefore remains more or less unfruitful. The right "interpretation" is missing. God has no chance. And at the same time, distance is also lacking. The distance comes about precisely because the deep level is connected, because the action flows forth from the soul's center, and because contact with the center is continually preserved. Thanks to this contact with the center, a perfect balance arises between the outward movement and the presence in itself that distinguishes man from animals.

Relaxation is a royal road to the deep level and to freedom; while at the same time the greatest relaxation is a consequence of the fact that one really lives reconciled with one's depths. The only one fully relaxed is the one who has let go of everything except this one thing: to be openness to God here and now.

Behold, I Am Doing a New Thing (Is 43:19)

The words "now" and "new", if not etymologically related, are however related to each other in reality. To live in the now makes life a wonderful adventure because everything that happens is always new.

Life is often nothing more than an eternal repetition. And what we call "experience" means, in many cases, that we have once and for all adopted a definite pattern of action that we repeat for the rest of our lives. Often fifty years of experience is nothing more than a year's experience repeated fifty times. It is no wonder life is boring!

"Behold, I make all things new" (Rev 21:5). Every moment in your life can be new because every moment is *newly* created by God. To create means to bring into existence out of nothing. Surely you have your conditions that more or less externally direct your life. But the horizontal view is not the whole truth. Every moment binds you vertically with your Creator, who always creates you anew in the present moment. At every moment, he offers you the chance to do something completely new with the perhaps formless and, above all, formable mass that makes up your past.

What is decisive is not what your conditions are but how you make use of them. The exterior frame of your life, formed by what you have inherited, your environment, and all your previous experiences and decisions, seems to limit your freedom and force you into a boring monotony. But deeper than the exterior frame, there is a freedom you have to choose: how you will respond to the challenge of the exterior framework. You never stumble here on any definite limitations. You can continuously mature and grow in the art of giving new answers to old questions.

God, who is the Omega, the end and goal of everything, is always the Alpha, the beginning (cf. Rev 21:6). He is always "in the beginning" (Gen 1:1, Jn 1:1). We mostly think of "the beginning" as a fixed point in *time*. We ought rather to see it as a determination of a state or situation. With God, there can never be anything old. He creates everything *now*.

To distinguish between *creatio* (to create) and *conservatio* (to sustain) is bad creation theology. To live is never to "sustain" something in being. To live is always *to begin anew*.

Today is the first day of the rest of your life.

An Unfruitful Now

But there is also a bad "momentariness". Gabriel Marcel, whom I have already quoted, speaks of *instantanéisme*, a way of living for the moment, of being totally taken up in the "actual moment".

That is particularly the mass media's unhappy "charism", to make us live for the moment. Via the mass media, I am able to see and hear everything that is happening "now". But that now can easily become empty and unfruitful because it is taken out of its context.

There is no longer contact with the past or the future and, least of all, with God. The vertical dimension is completely absent, and the horizontal is so hollowed out that one could speak of an emaciated now, a now without any vitality.

That explains why we often have a feeling of powerlessness when we look at television. The flood of news pours over us. Everything terrible and tragic that has happened in the world is concentrated in a news broadcast of a few minutes. But no one speaks of the challenges and hidden possibilities of these events. What the people who are suffering misfortune *make of their fate* is not told, nor can it be said.

The consequence is that we get a picture of reality that is askew. The reality we see on the TV screen has little to do with the reality that God is creating now. The deep dimension of reality is missing, and what is left is only an empty shell of it.

But rather than blame the mass media, we ought to blame our way of using them. If we are far too generous with the time we give to the media, there comes the risk that we no longer see the forest for the trees, that despite the fact that we have seen or heard everything, we do not know about what is *actually happening*.

One can also live in an empty now while one is working. To lose a feeling for time is not an infallible sign that one is living in God's eternal now! One can drown in one's work, lose "one's soul" in it. Perhaps we have a feeling that time stands still. But time probably also stands still for the cat that runs after the mouse.

Without the distance I mentioned, there is not typically human action. And the "timelessness" one eventually experiences comes from the fact, not that one lives in the present moment, but that one is escaping oneself in the work.

There is a now that is miserably poor, uninteresting, and sterile, even if it gives enjoyment and satisfaction for the moment. Hans Urs von Balthasar speaks of a timeless "now", without it being past or future, a kind of *negative eternity* due to the absence of God.[10] "All things are twofold, one opposite the other", says Jesus Sirach (42:24). The positive eternity responds to the negative.

The positive, genuine now is not an island, not a "monad" without either doors or windows (Leibniz, 1646–1716). The past and the future are contained in the positive now. It is a synthesis of all the dimensions of time. Your memories and hopes are contained in the now and expand it. In the present, you meet your past, which asks of you: Create me anew! Transform me! And in the present moment, you lay the foundation for your future. Is there a better way to prepare for your future than by wholeheartedly consenting to the work given to you now?

The present moment is the gateway to eternity. And eternity contains *everything*.

---

[10] *La mission ecclésiale d'Adrienne von Speyr*, Actes du colloque romain (Paris: Lethielleux, 1986), 157: "une sorte d'éternité négative de la perte de Dieu".

13

The Eternal Pulses
in the Midst of Time

Eternity has been unpopular for a long time. Did eternity not belong to the well-known opium that was thought to anesthetize the person and hinder him from being engaged in time and giving himself to his mission in the world? Even if Marxism has seen its better days, we are still influenced by its thought patterns. We are afraid of an escape from reality. There is enough to do here in time. Is it not wiser to do what can be done *now* than to dream of an uncertain eternity?

Such reflections suggest an erroneous understanding of eternity.

What Is Eternity?

First, let us see what eternity is *not*.

Eternity is not unlimited time. That is how we surely imagine eternity in general. We think of it as a time that has neither a beginning nor an end. God lives and reigns "from eternity to eternity". There is no border either to the left or to the right.

If we understand God's eternity in that way as end-less time, we make him very small. As we have seen, what characterizes time is that one thing follows after the other. Time means change, development. To live in time, then, means to *become*. But God *is*. There is no growth or maturation in him. He has and is all at once. Man grows old by the fact that he lives in time. God's eternity, on the other hand, makes it so that he is always young. In God, there is no past or future. He lives in a permanent present.

Saint Thomas Aquinas quotes Boethius, who distinguishes between *nunc fluens* and *nunc stans*.[1] *Nunc fluens* (the fleeting, passing now) is a moment between what was and what is to come. This now passes away like water in a river. *Nunc stans* (the lasting, remaining now), on the other hand, is immovable. It is this latter now that characterizes God's being.

What distinguishes time is movement, change, fragmentation; while eternity is distinguished by stability, impenetrability, perfection. Time has often been likened to the base of a large mountain. The top of the mountain represents the unique moment of eternity. From the top of the mountain, God sees everything that happens in time with a single glance. He sees how generation after generation marches past. Or, one can think of Mozart (1756–1791), who is said to have had whole symphonies in his head, which he later wrote down "in time".

---

[1] Saint Thomas Aquinas, *Summa Theologica* I, q. 10, a. 2, ad 1.

Eternity is associated by many people with boredom. In an immovable now, there is no room for exciting discoveries. When everything is concentrated in a single moment, nothing new can happen anymore. The same people often find difficulties with the promise of heaven. How can we be happy in heaven when for all eternity we will have nothing else to do but sing "holy, holy, holy"? But does this need for variation and change not spring from the fact that we are unsatisfied? That something is still missing? When all gaps are filled and all needs satisfied, one no longer chases after something new.

It is precisely because God is eternal that he is so serene and peaceful. In meeting him, we are allowed to taste something of eternity, and the needs of time become uninteresting. It is then we say: "Whom have I in heaven but you? And there is nothing upon earth that I desire besides you" (Ps 73:25), none of the limited satisfactions time can give.

Because we so often pray that our dead may "rest in peace", we have a tendency to associate rest and peace with death. But God's rest is not the rest of death but the total harmony of the perfect life. What we usually call the "prayer of quiet" is quiet only because for a moment we are able to taste that eternity where there is no more dissatisfaction.

The Antithesis of Eternity:
The Fleetingness of Time

"Time passes quickly, time flies", we often say. What strikes us most when we think of time is its fleetingness. Everything passes on this earth. Events are like clouds that glide past. Sometimes, when life feels wonderful, we would like to say with Faust: "verweile doch, du bist so schön" (stay a while, you are so beautiful). But time is merciless. It goes its way without caring about our wishes.

Especially when we look back in time, it seems as though it has rushed along at a tremendous speed. The child thinks that Grandma has lived an endlessly long life, and the thought of getting that old is dizzying: it is as though one had an eternity ahead. But Grandma herself remembers her childhood as though it were yesterday, and her whole life seems to her like a fleeting dream.

Everything is gone. Nothing is left.

"All those things have vanished like a shadow,
and like a rumor that passes by;
like a ship that sails through the billowy water,
and when it has passed no trace can be found,
nor track of its keel in the waves;
or as, when a bird flies through the air,
no evidence of its passage is found;
the light air, lashed by the beat of its pinions

and pierced by the force of its rushing flight,
is traversed by the movement of its wings,
and afterward no sign of its coming is found there;
or as, when an arrow is shot at a target,
the air, thus divided, comes together at once,
so that no one knows its pathway.
So we also, as soon as we were born, ceased to be."
(Wis 5:9–13)

Who has not experienced sadness over the fact that everything passes and that the greater part of life is over? The past in my life becomes ever greater, the future ever smaller. It seems as though the past is swallowing the future. In the end, there is only the past that is left, the unreal, the dream.

In principle, it is not true that a person "has" time. Time slips away like sand between our fingers. We have no power over it. It is out of our reach.[2] It can seem as though time is moving toward us. It comes and moves closer. But as soon as it arrives, it has already gone. Time is as slippery as an eel. We can never get a grip on it. It slips away, inexorably.

Naked time, that is, time that is stripped of its eternal dimension, is a curse. It plays hide and seek with us against our will.

But we should also be able to play along, voluntarily. And this would perhaps be a way of breaking the curse of time. We can *let* time fly; we can flow with

[2] Cf. Benkt-Erik Benktson, *Samtidighetens mirakel, Kring tidsproblematiken I Lars Gyllenstens romaner* (Stockholm: Bonniers, 1989), 78, 81.

the stream. After all, why should we try to stop its speed? We are longing for "a better country, that is, a heavenly one" (Heb 11:16). "For here we have no lasting city, but we seek the city which is to come" (Heb 13:14). And time brings us there! If time did not pass, or if it passed more slowly, the waiting time would be so much longer. Would we prefer the prelude to the symphony?

The passing of time can become a blessing to the one who, like Saint Paul, forgets what lies behind and stretches toward that which lies ahead and races on toward the finish line (Phil 3:13–14). Yes, time itself seems to hurry along and be impatient. It does not stand still for a moment but hastens toward the goal.

Perhaps the fleetingness of time is nothing more than its speedy eagerness to reach that moment when it will dissolve in eternity.

The Eternal Dimension of Time

But is time really naked? Is it not man himself who has "unrobed" time and so made it to be merely passing? There is an eternal moment built into time. Time is clothed with eternity.

Instead of thinking of time and eternity as two horizontal lines that run parallel and therefore never meet, we ought to see eternity as a vertical line that is in constant contact with time. The vertical line of eternity stands still, while time moves horizontally. Time is touched by eternity at every moment, and that contact gives time a deep dimension.

"We discussed something about time and eternity", writes Hjälmar Ekström in a letter, "of how every point in time is affected by eternity, when we no longer can get a grip on time or on that which is seen, heard, and perceived in an external way. When we let go, we are then taken hold of by eternity and are carried in God's bosom."[3]

Man knew already in antiquity that there was something eternal and fixed in changing reality. Plato's (427–347 B.C.) philosophy is an attempt to explain why man, in his best moments, believes he experiences something of the absolute in this changing world. The world of the senses is not all of reality. But while Plato's ideas form a world of their own, raised high above the changing world that we comprehend with our senses, the New Testament reveals a greater realism. The eternal truth is not far away but in the midst of our reality. The eternal dimension is a fundamental element in the reality in which we live.

This was so already in the plan of creation. Everything is created not only by God but *in* God. "In him all things were created, in heaven and on earth" (Col 1:16). We have our origin in God, and it is in him we live and move and have our being (Acts 17:28–29). He is the inner light that enlightens every man

[3] Hjälmar Ekström, *Den fördolda verkstaden* (Lund: Gleerup, 1963; new ed.: Skellefteå: Artos, 1988), 32.

(Jn 1:4, 9). The traditional theologian speaks of God's substantial presence in everything that exists. By his act of creation, God lets everything created participate in his own being. He is the indwelling principle that guides everything created toward its goal.

Every believer *knows* that this is so. But even one who does not believe in God, provided that he does not let himself be blinded by the constant fluctuation of things and events, can have an idea of and even to some extent experience a deep dimension that makes time related to eternity. There is a certain *trans-historical depth* in history, says Gabriel Marcel.

When we have learned to see creation with this deep gaze, the perishableness of created things need not cause us sorrow. The purer our gaze becomes, *the more we are freed from demands and desires*, the more clearly we see the eternal substance shine forth through everything.

When it is a question of my own "history", it is easy to see that it is not reduced to a series of random events. I can discover "the thread" that connects all the different events in my life. This deep dimension does not lie far away. To discover it does not require any deep concentration. It is just by letting go, by detaching myself from all "straining", that I can lay hold of it. When I do not try to capture and hold fast to the perishable dimension, I become free to see the eternal.

What is true for my personal history is also true for the history of mankind. A historian can content himself with enumerating facts and data. But he can also describe history as a dynamic process. He sees that mankind, despite all its detours and regressions, is on the way toward a goal. He does not see facts but development. The one who seeks union with God also realizes ever more "the Sacred History" where God, in a sovereign way, lets everything that happens serve his purposes to lead us all to an eternal union of love with him and each other.

The anthropic principle in physics, according to which the cosmos as a whole develops in the direction of the human person and finds its perfection in him, is an expression of man's victory over time that passes away. This anthropic principle reveals something of time's deep or eternal dimension. We find this dimension already in Saint Paul: "All things were created . . . for him" (Col 1:16), that is, for Christ, the perfect, divine man. By the fact that everything is directed to him, everything receives its meaning, and all becomes one.

But for the one who does not believe and trust in anything eternal and "fixed" in the changing reality, history becomes an aimless and meaningless event.

The Church prays in one of the Collects of the Mass that "amid the uncertainties of this world, our hearts may be fixed on that place where true gladness is found."[4] "Lift up your hearts", the priest says during the Mass. This is something we can do continuously: lift up our hearts from the limited, perishable level of

---

[4] Collect, Twenty-First Sunday in Ordinary Time.

creation to the eternal and lasting, where all beauty, goodness, and truth have their origin. We do not need to leave creation for this; we need only to see it in its true reality.

The eternal pulsates in the midst of time. In the deepest depths, the grip of time is dissolved, and everything is gathered into a unity that never passes away.

Perishable Time and Christ Time

How could time be naked, merely fluctuating and passing away, when the Eternal One has stepped into time and made a covenant with it? In Christ, time and eternity form a perfect synthesis. God, who lives beyond time, enters into our human history, becomes bound by time, but without ceasing to be God. He shows us that, against all expectations, it is not impossible for God to live in time and, above all, that it is not impossible for man to live in eternity. He reveals the forgotten secret we bear within us: that our inmost being is a door to eternity. The more Christlike we become, the more the door already opens in our existence here.

Everything Jesus did during his earthly life has eternal value because everything flows out from his center where he is rooted in the Father. This nucleus of eternity never leaves him; it is his essence. When he speaks of death, the clearest symbol of perishable time, it is only in order to say that he has conquered it. Every allusion to his death ends in a triumphant "and on the third day he shall rise again."

Through faith in Christ and by seeking communion with him in prayer, we become one with his way of living in time. We become, as Søren Kierkegaard says, contemporary with him. This becomes concretely expressed and clear in the sacraments. By eating his Body and drinking his Blood in the Eucharist, we become present, but "present" is too weak a word; we ought to say "indwelling", when he transforms his death into a voluntary giving of his life. We can tangibly experience that death itself becomes life. And we dare to make the Psalmist's words our own: "I shall not die, but I shall live" (Ps 118:17).

To know him who is from the beginning, to do his will, is to last forever (1 Jn 2:13–14, 17).

Faith in Christ can be more or less strong. A half-hearted faith does not lead to an experience of liberation. How could it? But for the one to whom faith has become "whole", the roots of his personality have been transplanted, or rather they have finally taken root in the soil for which they were created and where eternity surrounds them on all sides. There, one's own limited personality is in some way taken out of the picture. It is God's territory, where he is everything and where man is "lost" in him. This is the substance of eternal life that firmly is and shall remain.

"He is like a tree planted by streams of water, that yields its fruit in its season, and *its leaf does not wither*" (Ps 1:3; emphasis added). Death is no longer corruptibility that has the upper hand but, rather, a door that opens.

All of this is summed up in a clear text from Adrienne von Speyr (1902–1967):

> Passing time is an invention of God; he himself is in eternity. Time is measured by the measure of man and his life: The world always remains one generation until the time when the Son of God takes upon himself a lifetime from this time, borrows thirty-three years from man's lifetime in order to live through them. But because he has borrowed them from man, he gives back to man *his* time, which is an unfragmented eternal time. The end of Jesus' earthly time is his death. But the dying Son turns the course of time back into the sphere of eternity, so that man shall be able to share in eternal life in time. As believers we live our time in an awareness of eternal time and must align our entire behavior to the eternal time that has been revealed to us through the Resurrection of the Son.[5]

Open Doors to Eternity

We can all have glimpses of eternity, whether we are believers or not. These glimpses are like "road signs": they show us the way; they show how it can be, how it should be. Experience, if ever so unassuming, usually means more to us than a great amount of abstract knowledge.

We have all experienced that *nature* is a door to eter-

---

[5] Barbara Albrecht, *Eine Theologie des Katholischen*, vol. 1 (Einsiedeln: Johannes Verlag, 1972), 53.

nity. What is special about nature is that it communicates a feeling of timelessness in the midst of the changes of time. The cloud glides past; the surface of the ocean rises and falls; it is evening and morning; everything is in motion, yet everything speaks of something that lies beyond motion, of an all-encompassing stillness in which every sound and movement has its place. Listen to the song of the hills; look at the billowing cornfield; open yourself to the fragrance of the blooming rapeseed flowers.

You do not need to be a mystic to understand that nature's message speaks of wholeness. Despite the fact that everything nature displays is fragmented, you experience—*if* you allow nature to be what it is— wholeness in every fragment. It is not difficult to meditate in nature, to dream of paradise. In untouched nature, the divine is so near.

Everything is created in God, visible and invisible, our own inner world and the creation around us. That is why we so easily find rest and peace in nature. Our (perhaps unconscious) intuition tells us we are at home and that we can be ourselves in nature: it and we have the same origin. And we know intuitively that this origin is eternal and that we, together with all of creation, are on the way back there.

Many find it easier to see the "traces" of God in nature than in their fellowmen. Our Nordic Psalm poets are masters in perceiving and communicating nature's eternal ring. They actually do nothing more than build further on a tradition that is as old as man.

Oh, when so much beauty is revealed in every vein
of creation and life,
how beautiful must the source itself be, the eternal
bright One![6]

Man has always known that nature speaks a mysterious language. But it is not so mysterious that it cannot be deciphered even by a secularized person if he
is able to leave his cigarettes and his smartphone at
home.

Is there not a resonance in us when we read Saint
John of the Cross' poems and hear how he asks the
question of creation:

> O woods and thickets,
> Planted by the hand of my Beloved!
> O green meadow,
> Coated, bright, with flowers,
> Tell me, has He passed by you?

And then when creation answers:

> Pouring out a thousand graces,
> He passed these groves in haste;
> and having looked at them,
> with His image alone,
> clothed them in beauty.[7]

---

[6] J. O. Wallin, *I Psalmbokens ekumeniska del*, no. 305, 5.

[7] Saint John of the Cross, *The Spiritual Canticle*, stanzas 4, 5,
in *The Collected Works of Saint John of the Cross*, trans. Kieran
Kavanaugh, O.C.D., and Otilio Rodriguez, O.C.D. (Washington, D.C.: ICS Publications, 1991), 495–96.

Another door to eternity is to *live in reality*.

Are we not doing that? Is it not something obvious? No. Instead of living in reality, we often live in our thoughts, prejudices, illusions, and our fixed, unchangeable mental structures. Reality seldom has a chance to reach us in its original freshness. We project our "prefabricated" ideas and conceptions onto reality. What we see is, not reality, but our idea of reality.

The only solution is to let go of ourselves and open up to reality as it is in itself. We must learn to see people and things in a new way, as though we were seeing them for the first time. We need to learn to let them be what they are and not force them to be what they are not but only what we imagine them to be. We make everything so small when we lock it into our old preconceptions. Reality is greater. According to ancient philosophy, everything that *is* witnesses to the One Who Is. Real contact with reality gives us a perception of the infinite.

This is especially clear in our interpersonal relationships. If I go to meet a person with this new, fresh, open gaze, I experience him as a mystery. He is always more than what I know about him. To approach him with the attitude: "I know who you are" is to stifle him. A question mark is the only way that is right: "Who are you?" In this "always greater" that he represents, I meet a transcendent, eternal reality.

Every person I meet has something totally unique to communicate to me. If I am not open, I lose the chance of becoming more and greater. Only when I open myself to the transcendence and depth of the other can I reach deeper into my own depths. We are indispensable to each other. We are created as one single body.

But also during work time, in my tasks, I can experience something of eternity. When I give all of my attention to the task that is given to me at this moment without thinking of myself, of how much I will earn from it, or when it must be finished, I transcend time.

It is always self-absorption, the thought of our own interests, that holds us as prisoners of time. The moment that we let go and open up to reality, we leave that prison.

To live in reality creates inner peace. And the reverse is also true: without a certain inner peace and silence, it is impossible to live in reality. For the one who lives in an inner silence, everything speaks a language of eternity. Even "the clocks tick eternity."[8] Noise bears the mark of that which perishes; silence, that of eternity. The Eternal One is not in the storm or the earthquake, but in the "still small voice" (1 Kings 19:11-13). In silence we have the chance to come closer to our deepest center, which is an ocean of peace and calm, where nothing of all that moves in time is excluded but is only transformed into eternity. There

[8] Ingemar Leckius, *Vid Terebint Trädet* (Stockholm: Bonniers, 1989), 33.

it is never a question of "doing" but only of "being".

Man is not created to have but to be, as Pope John Paul II often said in his speeches and homilies.

About merely being, Hjälmar Ekström writes some beautiful lines:

> Look at the violets, how they stand and hide from everyone's gaze, far from the need to make an impression on others. They hardly wish to admit that they are flowers, and yet they reveal both color and scent, unconscious of themselves. That is how it is in God's garden. There, no words of time are spoken; there, no deeds of time are done; there, no one stands out among others, for such belongs to time. No, there the words of eternity are spoken, the silent and hidden, which can only speak by remaining silent and standing still before God.[9]

But *love* is the *true* door to eternity. If we open it, all the other doors open of themselves.

For a believer, this is not so remarkable. "God is love, and he who abides in love abides in God, and God abides in him" (1 Jn 4:16). Nevertheless, even the one who does not believe, if he cannot understand, he can at least intuit that there is an absoluteness, a moment of eternity in love. "To love someone is to say: you will never die", writes Gabriel Marcel. If love is real love, that is to say, unlimited and unconditional, it

[9] Hjälmar Ekström, *Den stilla kammaren* (Skellefteå: Artos, 1988), 15.

transcends all circumstances, all "therefores". It rests in itself. It is its own source and goal.

Two people who are in love experience and know that their love transcends themselves, that it is more than the love of one plus the love of the other. In love, they touch a transcendent reality that stands outside of time and space. Love coincides with life itself. And how could love be able to die?

Everything that is not love, everything that is not given from ourselves, is marked by perishable time. There is always too little or too much time. We are stressed or bored. But if we forget ourselves and work for another, and thereby also for the Other (Mt 25:40), time receives a taste of eternity.

The Eucharist teaches us to offer bread and wine. Everything that is offered leaves the perishable sphere. The mystery of the nonperishable is these two words: "for you" (given, poured out).

The wonderful thing about it is that when we offer everything as a sacrifice and thereby leave perishable time, unending time is born, precisely as much as we need. If we compete with time, there is never enough of it. But if we do not care about it and we think only of working "for you", then it is never lacking. For the one who gives his work as an offering, the quantity of time is never a problem. Here, too, it is a question of the fact that the Heavenly Father knows what we need (Mt 6:32).

We are created for love, to be an image of God as

a Trinitarian communion of love. This is our eternal life. Every little spark of love is at the same time a spark of eternal life that is given to us already here and now.

"O love, who are eternal life in the changeableness here. . . ."[10]

[10] N. F. S. Grundtvig and E. Liedgren, *I Psalmbokens ekumeniska del*, no. 258, 7.

14

The Church's Time

When God sends his Son, time is "fulfilled" (Mk 1:15, Gal 4:4). But this fulfillment does not mean that time is finished. This very fulfillment is a process.

The Old Testament, particularly the prophets, gives us an impression that all the promises will be realized at once when the Messiah comes. The New Testament nuances this perspective and shows that "the end" of time is not a point but a new era that has a certain time span. By the fact that Jesus has come, the essential has happened and history has, in a certain sense, reached its goal. But what Jesus has done must bear fruit, and that takes time. Jesus himself has pointed out that the kingdom has come (Lk 17:21) but that it is not yet fully grown. The kingdom is like a mustard seed or leaven.

There is a time, a short time (Jn 16:16), between Jesus' Ascension and his return. "This Jesus, who was taken up from you to heaven, will come in the same way as you saw him go into heaven" (Acts 1:11). This short time is the Church's time. What characterizes this time?

The Church Plays with the
Three Dimensions of Time

When we considered Christian time, we saw that it is a mysterious blend of time and eternity. This becomes particularly clear when we consider the Church's time. On the one hand, the Church takes the natural, cosmic time seriously. She even gives it a sacred meaning. It is the cosmic rhythms that decide the date of Easter. Every week begins with the "the Lord's Day", which allows the light from Christ's Resurrection to shine over all the days of the week. The people of the Church are born, grow up, mature, age, and die exactly as everyone else, and the Church leads them in these different periods of life with her sacraments and services. This dependence on the rhythm of time is not a "necessary evil". God has ordained it to be so. But God has also intended that this should not be the only dimension in which the Church lives because, on the other hand, the Church's time exhibits a sovereign independence from the natural course of time. The Church plays with the three dimensions of time and is comfortable with rearranging their natural order. The future does not necessarily come after the past but can just as well precede it. The Church moves back and forth through the past, present, and future with an amazing freedom. In this respect, she is indifferent to logic.

We have already spoken about the victory of the

Eucharist over the divisive power of time. The Eucharist is a memorial of Christ's death and Resurrection and points to a historic event. But at the same time, it anticipates the future; in the transformed Bread, which symbolizes the whole cosmos, everything is already subjected to the Son and incorporated into him (1 Cor 15:27-28). We who participate in the Eucharist in the present live the simultaneous dimensions of time at the same time. The past has not disappeared, and the future is not something for which we are only waiting, but, rather, everything is present *now*.

In Advent, we prepare for Christmas when we remember and celebrate the birth of Jesus, which occurred two thousand years ago. The past fills us with joy. But at the same time we turn our gaze back in time, we also look forward. Advent is also a longing for the return of Christ on the last day.

When we pray: "Come Lord Jesus", the Old Testament longing for the Messiah vibrates in these words. We feel united with the patriarchs and the prophets. But these words are also charged with the longing of the Christian Church for the fulfillment of history, when God will be all in all (1 Cor 15:28). We not only move back and forth between the past and the future, but we find ourselves in both at the same time.

We see this unusual blending of time's dimensions continuously in the Church's liturgy and life of prayer. Everything is multi-dimensional. In a famous Christmas sermon, Tauler (ca. 1300-1361) explains

that Christmas is the celebration of a triple birth: the
Son's eternal birth from the Father, Jesus' birth in Bethlehem, and Christ's birth in us. The first birth is outside of time; the second belongs to the past; and the
third is an on-going process.

During the liturgy of the Easter Vigil, the Church
invites us to a masterly synthesis of time's three dimensions. All of the important moments of salvation
history march past. It begins with creation and ends in
heaven. In the Liturgy of the Word, we hear how God
saved his people in past ages. Seven key texts from the
Old Testament allow us to walk through the entire
Old Covenant. But the Letter to the Romans (6:3–11)
proclaims that Christ has been raised from the dead
and that death no longer has power over him. And the
text ends with this triumphant statement: "So you also
must consider yourselves dead to sin and alive to God
in Christ Jesus."

In the liturgy of baptism and in the renewal of our
baptismal vows, each one of us who participates in
the liturgy lives through this synthesis tangibly. To go
down or be immersed in the water is to die to the old
man: the past is drowned in God's mercy. To rise up
from the water is to be born to a new life that flows
out into eternal life. All of this happens in one and the
same act. Here, time's fragmentation is overcome. The
different phases of time flow together into one single
point.

In its liturgy and prayer life, the Church finds herself on different levels at the same time. These dif-

ferent planes cross each other without interruption. This makes the Church's time immensely rich but also mysterious. The one who wants clear, exact answers can feel frustrated. What are you really talking about, Bethlehem or the final judgment? The Church speaks of everything at once.

In reality, this is not so unusual. The Church's time is marked by Jesus' time. And he juggles past, present, and future tenses and mixes them. Before Abraham *was*, I *am* (Jn 8:58; emphasis added). He is born of the Father "before all time". He is the center of history and the heart of the world, and he is at the same time the Omega; the absolute future. The one who lives in him—and the Church does this—has entrance into all of history at once and even transcends history. Everything converges in him who *is*.

The Past Is Here and Now

The past is never irreversibly gone. Since this is one of the main themes of this book, and we also have an in-built resistance to such a thought, I allow myself once more to bring it out. The current understanding that "done is done" is not correct, least of all for the one who lives in step with the Church's time.

I do not need to grieve over my past and believe there is nothing I can do about it. Thanks to the sacramental life of the Church, I have access to my past. It is always at my disposal. In some way, it is more at my disposal now than when it happened. Distance allows me to see the past now in its whole perspective. I can see the place it has in my life and how it actively helps to "give my life purpose" and plays a positive role in my development. Wounds caused by sin can become wounds of love, says Saint John of the Cross.[1]

I remember a retreat from my high school days. The priest began with some words that became engraved in my memory: "Timeo dominum transeuntem et non revertentem" (I fear the Lord who passes by and who does not come again). It was not difficult for me to understand the meaning. A retreat is a chance for conversion. If you miss this chance, it is definitively lost. It will never come back.

Later, I realized that this is not the whole truth and that it can even be dangerous to overemphasize the unique character of such a chance. God not only passes by, he also comes back, not only because there are new opportunities to make a retreat, but because the very missed opportunity can in some way be brought back or recovered. I can return to my past and transform it, not in its external reality, but in its substance.

When I receive forgiveness for my sins in the Church, my past becomes "transubstantiated". We underestimate forgiveness when we understand it to mean only a wiping away of our sins. Forgiveness does much more than that. It recreates our past. The lamentation is trans-

[1] Saint John of the Cross, *The Living Flame of Love*, stanza 2, no. 7, in *The Collected Works of Saint John of the Cross*, trans. Kieran Kavanaugh, O.C.D., and Otilio Rodriguez, O.C.D. (Washington, D.C.: ICS Publications, 1991), 660.

formed into a song of praise: "He put a new song in my mouth, a song of praise to our God" (Ps 40:3).

The Future Is Here and Now

Just as I can freely move back and forth between the past and the present, so also do I have access to the future. In the Church, the future is not far away; it is here and now.

Through my baptism, an event that occurred many years ago, I have once and for all been "marked" by my future. Past and future meet and kiss one another in baptism. In and through baptism, I have received my true, eternal identity. "We were buried therefore with him by baptism into death, so that as Christ was raised from the dead by the glory of the Father, we too might walk in newness of life" (Rom 6:4). My true identity is Jesus Christ: "For as many of you as were baptized into Christ have put on Christ" (Gal 3:27).

"Dare to be who you are in Christ", is a song we sing in Church. And it continues, "you already are who you shall one day be; judged and pardoned, dead and risen, loved and made one with him who has made you free."[2]

The desire for the future can easily be an escape from the present moment. We are experts in being nonchalant about what we have and focus on what we do not have. Is it often not easier to love those who are far away than to love those who are near? What

[2] A. Frostenson, *I Psalmbokens ekumeniska del*, no. 87, 1 and 4.

lies completely within our reach does not seem especially exciting. And you do not need to long for it.
You can receive it and rest in it. If you wish to desire
something, you can desire to "dare to be who you are
in Christ."

Hjälmar Ekström writes that "every step of the
way", you can "arrive at the perfect goal". "For the
goal is his embrace, and in it you are carried just as
much during the journey to the goal as at the arrival."[3]

But are we not sinners? As long as we let ourselves
be carried in his arms, as long as we expose ourselves
to his loving gaze, sin has no power over us. "But I
did not see sin, for I believe that it has no kind of substance, no share in being", writes Julian of Norwich
(1342–ca. 1416).[4] Sin is only a bad dream. The thing is
that man clings to this dream. God's eyes are too pure
to see evil. Before him, it cannot have any existence.
When we expose ourselves to his gaze, we become
immaculate.

If only we could understand how easy the "trick"
is to be washed clean constantly: one merely exposes
oneself completely to God's gaze. When we place ourselves stripped before him, we become captured by his
gaze. And sin and death no longer exist.

If you are pure creation, nothing more than creation wide open for him, then you have "arrived".

---

[3] Hjälmar Ekström, *Den fördolda verkstaden* (Lund: Gleerup,
1963; new ed.: Skellefteå: Artos, 1988), 80.

[4] Julian of Norwich, *Showings* (New York: Paulist Press, 1978),
chap. 27, p. 225.

The present and the future coincide. "Suddenly the soul is united to God, when she is truly pacified in herself", writes Julian also.[5] It is not by striving to be someone else but by letting God penetrate you with his loving gaze that you recover that original purity. That is precisely what purity is: not hiding anything from God.

In the Church's time, one thing does not follow *after* the other, but everything is simultaneous. In the Church, we have the great freedom of wandering back and forth unhindered between the past, the present, and the future. Nothing is inaccessible.

[5] Ibid., chap. 49, p. 265.

15

The Synthesis of the Liturgy

Saint Paul writes to the Philippians: "I do not consider that I have made it my own" (3:13). But almost immediately after that he says: "Let those of us who are mature" (v. 15). We are not perfect, but, nevertheless, we are. We have not arrived, and yet we have. We live in time, but also in eternity.

Seized by God

The explanation lies in what Saint Paul says to the Philippians in verse 12, "But I press on to make it my own, because Christ Jesus has made me his own." That I have been grasped by Christ means that the decisive event has already occurred: God's kingdom is here. I am clothed in Christ. *I am his.* But this ontological reality must be accepted; it must be integrated into my way of thinking, feeling, and acting. I wish to do everything to "grasp" it, so that I can say: *you are mine.*

"The end of the ages has come" upon us (1 Cor 10:11). A Christian is no "seeker". He knows that God has found him. After that, he does not need to "search" anymore. The only thing that remains is to let this knowledge penetrate the different layers of his consciousness.

My own experience, and that of others with whom I have been able to share, have taught me that life becomes different, that a person is filled with a new security, peace, and joy when he finally dares to believe that he is grasped by God. Even prayer, and perhaps especially prayer, goes through a metamorphosis. While you earlier sought God with much effort, often without finding him, you now rest in a certainty that you have long ago been "found" by him. Prayer is now mainly his doing. The burden is no longer yours. All your striving to meet God and be united with him is now superfluous. You do not strive toward the goal when you know you have reached it. Instead of striving to move forward, you can now move forward by resting.

Previously it was a torment when you were distracted and not concentrated in prayer. Since prayer was something you did yourself, a distracted prayer seemed like a failure. There was the thought of giving up everything: What sense is there to spend twenty minutes in interior prayer when nineteen of those minutes are spent "somewhere else"? But now, when you *know* that God has you in his grasp and that prayer is to rest in that, you are not as discouraged when you are distracted and lack concentration. You belong to God anyway. That which is, is and remains.

By resting in what is, you come to a deeper level in yourself besides, where thoughts are not as important. Perhaps the thoughts continue to wander, but

you are not completely in them. The rest, that dif-
fuse consciousness that you are in God's hand and that
everything is good, can remain, independent of the
thoughts. You prove your faithfulness to God's gift
by not "going into" the thoughts and calmly directing
them toward God again when you become conscious
that they are drifting about.

For the one who "seeks" God, joy is something that
occurs "sometimes" or "often", namely, every time he
"finds" God. But for a person who knows he is grasped
by God, joy is a spring that *always* flows. To be grasped
by God is to be grasped by Joy—a joy that is not di-
minished by human pain or earthly sorrow.

In Christ, God has come to stay. All of history was
directed toward this. That which comes later does not
actually come "after" this. In Christ, the fullness has
come (Col 1:19). Time seems to stand still. What remains of time is like the half-hour of silence of which
the Book of Revelation speaks (8:1). Eternity has begun before time has completely come to an end.

The prayerful person comes to experience this more
and more deeply.

The Liturgy as a Synthesis
of Time and Eternity

We are on the way to a goal we have already reached.

The Church is ingenious in her way of formulat-
ing this paradox. In her liturgy, time and eternity are
inseparable companions. There we concretely experience that time and eternity are not opposites of each

other, but that they can lovingly exist together. In the liturgy, we do not leave time: what we celebrate are historical events. But this does not prevent the Church from leading us into eternity.

It begins even with the church building. A church is built by people. It takes "time" for it to be built. The material that is used does not differ from what is used to make other buildings. Everything is marked by time and space. And nevertheless, when the building is finished, it is a gate to heaven and a place where God's glory dwells. "Here is foreshadowed the mystery of the true Temple, here is prefigured the heavenly Jerusalem."[1] And the one who enters it breathes eternity.

The church bells that ring for the *times* of worship services make eternity almost "audible". Their ringing, which combines seriousness with festive joy, can awaken a whole village out of banality and unite it in a context of timelessness.

Historical events that seemed doomed to perish and be lost reveal their eternal dimension in the Church's rituals. That which *once was* appears now as that which always is. Episodes that occurred at different times are brought together and become present in the now. Christ's death, his descent into hell, his Resurrection and Ascension, and his return in glory are all celebrated in one and the same worship service.[2] The beginning

---

[1] Mass for Dedication of a Church and an Altar, *The Roman Missal* (Yonkers, N.Y.: Magnificat, 2011), 1228.

[2] See the Fourth Eucharistic Prayer in the liturgy of the Catholic Mass.

of salvation history in the liturgy is not separated from its end. Christ's birth and death become simultaneous with each other and us. Everything that Jesus experienced, everything that happened to him during his earthly life, he has taken with him into his glory. It is this "total" Christ who comes to us in the liturgy. We encounter the fullness.

Every Eucharist shows us that eternity is present in everything that exists. "Your immortal spirit is in all things" (Wis 12:1). The bread and wine that are used in the Mass represent the whole cosmos. Christ's presence under the form of bread and wine implies that *all* things are filled with a divine presence, yes, that the whole cosmos is on the way to becoming his Body.

One of the liturgy's typical features is repetition. It makes an important contribution in conveying the experience of eternity. That the same prayers come back and are repeated day after day in the Church's Mass and the Liturgy of the Hours, that certain prayers themselves consist of repetition ("Lord have mercy", "Lamb of God"), allows us to realize something of the peace of eternity. Man's words are marked by the passing of time. But the repetition gives them a fullness and a power that is like eternity. Everyone who has some experience of prayer—and love—knows that one becomes more easily *recollected* when one often repeats the same words than if one is constantly creating new ones. Eternity is just that; that everything is *gathered* into one single point.

Out in society, life is marked by multiplicity, desire for variation. The liturgy, on the other hand, is characterized by simple repetition of the same words and the same gestures. In the world, everything is in movement, everything is changing, and time flies by. The Church is at home with simplicity and repetition. There time stands still. There the distance between the earthly and the heavenly liturgy is also bridged. The holy city, the new Jerusalem, has come down out of heaven (Rev 21:2). In the present, we anticipate our final future: to worship him who lives forever and ever and lay our crowns before his throne (Rev 4: 10).

Even the pictures and paintings of the saints and icons make us feel transported into eternity. Past time and future time flow together. We are at the same time with the saints of old and with the end time's apotheosis. Icons especially convey the experience of an all-encompassing now. That John the Baptist holds his head on a platter in front of him, while at the same time he still has it on his body, is only unusual for the one who is living in perishable time. The Church does not care about the logic of this age. She sees events and things from God's perspective, and for him, everything is happening simultaneously.

The Rhythm of the Church Year

"In my contacts with psychiatrists, psychotherapists, and psychologists", writes Helge Brattgård, "I have heard that the rhythm of the liturgical year gives both variation and stability to a person's understanding of

time and helps to alleviate the feeling of meaningless routine that often characterizes the existence of
many."[3]

The Old Covenant already had its "liturgical year",
which gave the cosmic time a new content and a new
meaning. Israel knew that God was present always and
everywhere. It was unthinkable that something should
happen where he was not included. All of history was
considered from God's perspective. One recognized
his action in everything.

Israel's "liturgical year" followed the agrarian rhythm
of life: the harvest festival and feast of reaping gave
a concrete expression to the conviction that cosmic
time was also God's time. Later, these feasts received
a new and richer content: one remembered and celebrated the wonders God had done with his people.

All of God's miracles are united in Jesus, who establishes the New Covenant. Therefore, the Church
actualizes the life of Jesus from beginning to end in
her liturgical year, or rather, there is no end, "since he
always lives" (Heb 7:25) from the beginning until his
return in glory. The Church shows that she lives the
same life as Jesus. With him she lives in time and at
the same time outside of time.

For the one who follows the calm cadence of the
liturgical year, time is never experienced as empty. Essential things have occurred in time, and they continue
to occur, because what Jesus has said or done can never

[3] Helge Brattgård, *Kyrkan och Tiden I Människan och Tiden*, p. 51.

disappear (Mk 13:31). The play of eternity is acted out in the scene of time.

Restlessness lessens when we are constantly reminded of the greatness that comes to us and happens with us independently of what we accomplish. We live from feast day to feast day and learn that life is a feast, a first beginning of the wedding feast in heaven.

Easter is the feast of feasts. It is from and around it that the Church year is structured. The central truth is that the Lord is risen, and we will live with him. It is this more than anything else that makes us eternal beings. The triumphant Alleluia of Easter proclaims the victory of life over death. Easter says that we are immortal, that the seed of eternity has fertilized time.

Sunday

But since we are so forgetful when it is a question of what is most important, we celebrate Easter more than once a year. The Church makes every Sunday a small Easter feast.

Already in the New Testament, Sunday is called "the Lord's day" (Rev 1:10). Sunday, not the sabbath, is the day of worship for Christians, because the Resurrection of Jesus occurred on the day after the sabbath. Sunday is the day of Resurrection. On Sunday, everyone gathers to celebrate the Lord's death and Resurrection in the Eucharist, "until he comes" (1 Cor 11:26). Yes, on Sunday we also celebrate his return. When Jesus speaks of coming back after a "little while" (Jn

16:16), this can refer to both his Resurrection and his final coming on "the last day". That is why Sunday was already called the *eighth day* in the letter of Barnabas (ca. 130).[4]

Many Church Fathers will elaborate on this theme later. The number eight is considered by them to be perfection, the number of the Resurrection and eternal bliss. While the week is the time of this world, the eighth day is eternity's time. The week of creation flows out into the eighth day, which according to Saint Basil (ca. 330–379) is the sacrament of eternal life.

Eternal life is to "rest from . . . labors" and so enter "God's rest" (Heb 4:10). On Sunday, we experience some of this rest in advance. The sabbath rest plays a central role in the Old Testament. Man shall rest because God himself rests. The rest even forms the high point of his activity: "On the seventh day God finished his work which he had done" (Gen 2:2). God's rest is an essential element in his work of creation.

The sabbath is for Israel the day when one has "time" for God; when one is open and receptive to him. The sabbath is God's time (Ex 20:10). Work is not everything in the life of man, and the value of work is not judged by its results or its usefulness. Work receives its value from the fact that it is commissioned by God, a fact that one has discerned and discovered in silence. The one who works on the sabbath shows that he does not trust in God, who promised to give his

[4] *De apostoliska fäderna* (Stockholm: Svenska Kyrkans Diakonistyrelses Bokförlag, 1967), 162–63.

people food on the sabbath "without cost": "See! The
LORD has given you the sabbath, therefore on the sixth
day he gives you bread for two days; remain every man
of you in his place" (Ex 16:29). On the sabbath, one
receives a foretaste of eternal rest. Then the words of
the psalm are realized: "Return, O my soul, to your
rest; for the LORD has dealt bountifully with you" (Ps
116:7).

In the beginning, the only "rest" on Sunday was
the time one gave to the celebration of the Eucharist.
It was only when Constantine the Great (285–337)
decided that the feast day of the week that was considered a day of rest in the Roman Empire should fall
on the Christian Sunday that it took on the sabbath's
character of rest. Similar to the sabbath, Sunday also
became the day when one was free for God and entered into his rest, when one could say: "He only is
my rock and my salvation" (Ps 62:2). Time revealed
its eternal dimension on Sunday. To celebrate Sunday
was to say "Stop!" to one's activity and, instead, to be
completely disposed to hear the breath of eternity.

Saint Thérèse of Lisieux describes the mixture of joy
and melancholy that she experienced about Sunday:

> If the big feasts were rare, each week brought one
> that was very dear to my heart, namely Sunday! What
> a day Sunday was for me! It was God's feast day,
> and feast of *rest* . . . This *joyous* day, passing all too
> quickly, had its tinge of *melancholy*. I remember how
> my happiness was unmixed until Compline. During

this prayer, I would begin thinking that the day of *rest* was coming to an end, that the morrow would bring with it the necessity of beginning life over again, we would have to go back to work, to learning lessons, etc., and my heart felt the *exile* of this earth. I longed for the everlasting repose of heaven, that never-ending *Sunday* of the *Fatherland*![5]

What has become of our Sunday? Does it surprise us that we find it difficult to perceive eternity in time when we neglect the unique opportunity for this that Sunday offers us? To celebrate the liturgy, to place ourselves before the Eternal One and thus let ourselves be filled with eternity, is no longer self-evident in our secularized society, not even for Christians. If we neglect the liturgy, whose charism it is to join daily life with God's holiness and eternity, then even daily life loses the festive quality that it could and ought to have. It becomes merely ordinary and banal.

But even as a day of rest, Sunday is often overlooked. Can we call our hectic life of free time rest? We often replace professional work with other work that demands our energy to an even greater degree and thus blocks the possibilities for reflection and recollection.

To the New Evangelization, spoken of continually by Pope John Paul II and of which "post-Christian"

[5] Saint Thérèse of Lisieux, *Story of a Soul: The Autobiography of Saint Thérèse of Lisieux*, trans. John Clarke, O.C.D., 3rd ed. (Washington, D.C.: ICS Publications, 2002), Manuscript A, chap. 2, pp. 41–42.

Europe is in such flagrant need, belongs, not the least, the rediscovery of Sunday's role in the life of the Christian, both as the day of common worship and as an occasion of rest as a source of restoration and being created anew.

Epilogue

Heaven's Time

Does man make a definitive break with time when he dies? Is there no more time on the other side of the grave?

Most people answer that time is typical for our life here on earth and, therefore, necessarily ends when man "leaves time".

Is this not an all too simplified answer? Are we not all too fixed on that form of time we experience during our life on earth and, therefore, do we not blind ourselves to other possible forms of time? Perhaps what we have experienced of time is not the whole truth about time.

One of the main thoughts in this book is that time and eternity are not diametrically opposed. They do not exclude but, rather, include each other and stand in an indissolubly intimate relationship with each other, just as that which is created does with its Creator.

It is man's relationship with God—Love itself—that decides if time is subjected to corruption or if every moment is a drop out of the sea of eternity in which he is able to share and that, in the end, he will find again when, after this existence on earth, he is surrounded by "the sea" on all sides. All time, every moment that is lived in love, is everlasting, is *"eternal time"*.

It seems clear to me that the "eternal time" *remains* in heaven. To behold God, the Eternal One, can hardly be something static, unchangeable. For man, who is and remains a created, limited being, God is always greater. Man can always penetrate deeper into him, "go from beginning to beginning, through constant new beginnings, which never end" (Saint Gregory of Nyssa, ca. 330–395).

When Saint John the Apostle describes the heavenly Jerusalem in the Book of Revelation, he speaks of a city whose gates stand always open and to which all the glory of the earth is brought (Rev 21:25–26). Something *happens* there, and one event follows the other, and every event awakens a new song of praise and thanksgiving to God. That is time, but a "time" whose actual purpose is to give us more of God, the Eternal One.

"And I heard every creature in heaven and on earth and under the earth and in the sea, and all therein, saying, 'To him who sits upon the throne and to the Lamb be blessing and honor and glory and might for ever and ever!'" (Rev 5:13). Everything created sings the same song, but each one with its own voice. Nothing created is left out of this participation in the eternal song of praise, not even time. The perishable time will no longer exist, but the eternal time, the eternally continuous more, will become what our lives consist of.

Man can experience something of this "fellowship"

of time and eternity already here and now. What is decisive is the *attitude* he has taken to everything he encounters. With a person who is open, simple, and pure of heart, goodness and faithfulness shall meet, time and eternity will kiss (cf. Ps 85:10).

After having read this manuscript of mine, a Carmelite nun wrote the following poem, which I do not wish to withhold from the reader:

Father, time is your tender fatherly embrace
   carrying us
toward you. It is a still stream that quietly flows and
steadfastly keeps the same direction.
There is no way to avoid the passing of time.
We are captured by its grip, which determinately
leads us toward you. New moments constantly flow
   over us with
messages from your eternity. You gave birth to us in
time so that we could reach your depth, which is a
   bubbling
spring without end. The inner mystery of time is so
   we can grow
toward that which is always more, and the present
moment is your faithful servant that opens the gate to
   eternity.
Father, teach us to surrender ourselves in freedom and
   love to
time's supporting power; help us to see its deep
   meaning and that
your love is both the source and the goal. Amen.